METROL...

OLDHAM TO CHORLTON
including the Oldham Loop railway

The new face of the Oldham Loop. Bombardier M5000 unit number 3023 runs into the futuristic Central Park tram stop on a St Werburgh's Road to Oldham Mumps working on 14th June 2012, the second day of operation of the new Metrolink line. *(CR)*

© 2013 Venture Publications Ltd

ISBN 978 1905 304 530

Standard power for the Oldham Loop line in the latter days of steam, Stanier 2-6-4T number 42645 of Agecroft shed heads bunker first through Royton Junction on 18th June 1955 with a Rochdale to Manchester train. The station and the extensive marshalling yard are long gone and all that remains today is a plain track double line. *(PH)*

CONTENTS

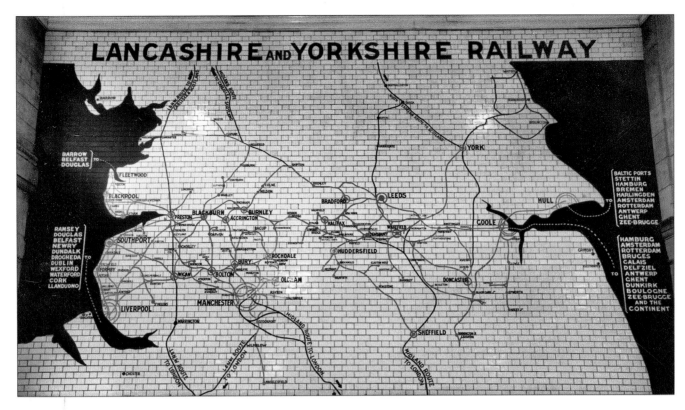

The famous wall map on the Victoria Station concourse. *(LYRS/NC)*

Lancashire and Yorkshire 2-4-2T number 253, by now LMS 10912, is pictured in July 1931 arriving at Victoria on a local train. The leading carriage is a former LYR Attock high-capacity coach, the remainder being standard LMS non-corridor stock. Note the ash ballast widely used on the Lancashire and Yorkshire which still existed at the time. *(LYRS/ERM)*

INTRODUCTION

Railways arrived in Rochdale in 1839, only nine years after the renowned Liverpool and Manchester Railway became the first intercity line. Three years later railways reached Oldham, but the link between Oldham Mumps and Rochdale was not opened until 1863, after several false starts. The direct route from Thorpes Bridge to Werneth took another seventeen years, opening in 1880. Thus was completed the line which became known in more recent times as the Oldham Loop.

The first railway was built by the Manchester & Leeds Railway (MLR) which, over time, acquired other railway companies and developed lines in the area becoming in 1847 the Lancashire and Yorkshire Railway (LYR). All the major developments of lines and services in the area were undertaken by the LYR. The context of the Oldham Loop in the LYR's full network in Manchester is shown below.

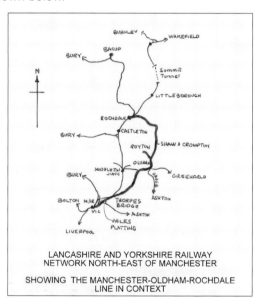

LANCASHIRE AND YORKSHIRE RAILWAY
NETWORK NORTH-EAST OF MANCHESTER

SHOWING THE MANCHESTER-OLDHAM-ROCHDALE
LINE IN CONTEXT

In 1922 the London and North Western Railway (LNW) merged with the LYR before the Grouping of Britain's railways in 1923. The lines under review then became the responsibility of the London Midland and Scottish Railway (LMS), the Central Division of which was based at the former LYR Head Office in Hunts Bank, Manchester. In 1948 the railways were nationalised and most of the LMS became the London Midland Region of British Railways

Responsibility for local railways was given to the South East Lancashire and North East Cheshire (SELNEC) Passenger Transport Authority (PTA), which was established on the 1st November 1969. The SELNEC Passenger Transport Executive (PTE) was the professional body responsible for planning the local integrated transport system. This responsibility was for service specification, future planning and finance of the local railways. The track and the trains, and associated staff, all continued to be owned or employed by British Railways, initially the London Midland Region, and more latterly the Regional Railways Sector, until the privatisation of British Railways (BR) in 1993. Following the separation of track and operations, Railtrack and, after its demise, Network Rail, became responsible for the rail infrastructure, including the control thereof, and operations were let to competitive franchisees.

The railways in the north were initially divided into two franchises: one covering the North West and the other covering the North East. The North West franchise was won by First North Western (Part of the First Group) who became responsible for the operation of the Manchester–Oldham–Rochdale services. Subsequently, the two franchises were re-combined into a Northern Franchise, which was won by a consortium of Serco and Netherlands Railways (subsequently re-named Abellio) which operated the Oldham Loop services until their closure for conversion in 2009. With local government reorganisation the Greater Manchester Passenger Transport Authority (GMPTA), an off-shoot of the Greater Manchester Metropolitan County Council (GMMCC), took over the responsibilities of the SELNEC PTA on 1st April 1974, the SELNEC PTE becoming the Greater Manchester PTE (GMPTE). Greater Manchester Council was abolished in 1986 and GMPTA became a joint authority of the ten Metropolitan District Councils. It was GMPTA/GMPTE which devised and developed the Metrolink system with the first tram operating from Bury to Manchester Victoria on 6th April 1992. Her Majesty the Queen opened the final part of Phase 1 on 17th July, 1992. The Eccles Extension opened in 1999 to Salford Quays (Broadway) and to Eccles in 2000.

Further reorganisation of responsibilities for public transport took place in 2011, when the Greater Manchester Combined Authority (GMCA) replaced the GMPTA (actually itself re-designated GMITA – the 'I' being for Integrated) for a short period. GMCA established a Transport for Greater Manchester Committee (TfGM) to look after transport affairs, including highways and car parking, the PTE becoming Transport for Greater Manchester's executive arm.

Phase 1 of Metrolink (Bury–City Centre–Altrincham) was constructed under a Design, Build, Operate and Maintain Contract (DBOM) by the GMA Group, a consortium made up of GECAlstom, John Mowlem and AMEC Civil Engineering. At a later stage Greater Manchester Buses (GMB), then still owned by GMPTE, joined the Consortium. The GMA Group established Greater Manchester Metro Ltd (GMML) to operate and maintain the Phase 1 system. Phase 2, the Eccles line, was built by ALTRAM, a consortium of the civil engineering firm of John Laing and Ansaldo, the parent group of Firema that built Manchester's original T68 trams for Phase 1. ALTRAM took over GMML. In due time ALTRAM gave up the contract and were replaced by Serco, a facilities management company, which took over operational and maintenance responsibility from GMML, the infrastructure being owned by the PTE but maintained by the operator.

Phase 3a was approved in May 2009 when GMPTA authorised a £1.5bn Special Fund for 15 transport projects, including the Metrolink 'Big Bang'. Three new contracts were drawn up and let by competitive tender: one to Design and Build (DB), a second to Operate and Maintain (OM) and a third to procure the rolling stock. The design and build of the extensions and the integration of the infrastructure was won in October, 2010 by MPact Thales Consortium. This consisted of Laing O'Rourke, Grant Rail and Thales UK. The OM Contract was won by Stagecoach, which became the partner responsible for operations and maintenance. Stagecoach is the operator of South Yorkshire Supertram, which took over from Serco on 15th July 2007. In a surprise move on 1st August 2011 Stagecoach sold its interest in Metrolink to RATP, the operator of public transport in Paris, and the new operator is MRDL. (Metrolink RATP Dpv Ltd). Interestingly, Stagecoach retained their ownership of Supertram in Sheffield. The rolling stock supply contract was won by Bombardier.

Work on the extended Metrolink system included building a new depot at Old Trafford which is now operational, with the original depot at Queens Road still being retained; building a line from Trafford Bar stop to St Werburgh's Road and building the East Manchester line from Piccadilly to Droylsden and later to Ashton. The link to Media City UK from Harbour City on the Eccles line was opened on 20th September 2010 to coincide with the start-up of the BBC's move to this location. A 12-minute off-peak service operates between Piccadilly and Media City. The section from St Werburgh's Road was opened on 7th July 2011 as the South Manchester line with the trams running to Victoria. It had been planned to extend this service to Central Park on the Oldham line in November, 2011, but this was postponed and the line was opened to a temporary terminus at Oldham Mumps on 13th June 2012.

Eventually, it is planned to operate a 6-minute frequency to Shaw and Crompton, and a 12-minute frequency to Rochdale. The new street-running Metrolink sections through Oldham Town Centre and from the railway station in Rochdale to the Town Centre interchange are both planned to open in 2014.

The Manchester-Oldham-Rochdale line nearly closed on several occasions from the sixties onwards, but managed to survive and even enjoyed improved services, thanks to the intervention of successive PTA's and PTE's and the efforts of STORM (Save the Oldham Rochdale Manchester line). Conventional rail services finally ceased in October 2009, but only to allow the line to be converted to Metrolink light rail or trams, as they are now recognised. This book tells the story of trains from Manchester to Oldham and Rochdale from 1839 and by the direct line through Hollinwood to Oldham from 1880. It covers the developments in railways north and east of Manchester, their operations, their survival against the odds and their conversion to Metrolink. It is hoped readers will enjoy this fascinating tale.

Scott Hellewell
Former Chief Planning Officer, SELNEC/GMPTE
Former Operations Director, Metrolink (GMML)

Colin Reeve
Former Operations & Planning Manager, GM Buses.

February 2013

New Metrolink boss arrives on schedule

- Peter Cushing to take on top role

- Chief arrives days before new line opens

DEAN KIRBY

>> DEPARTURE Philip Purdy is stepping down from his post and will be replaced by Peter Cushing (right)

A NEW Metrolink supremo is stepping into the driving seat as current boss Philip Purdy prepares to head back to his native Australia.

Mr Purdy will pass the baton to Peter Cushing, the former operations director of rail firm Central Trains.

Members of the Greater Manchester Combined Authority have given their backing to his appointment by Transport for Greater Manchester (TfGM).

It was revealed last summer that Mr Purdy, who took command of Metrolink in 2008, was preparing to step down from the £120,000-a-year role and return home for family reasons.

Mr Cushing has been working as interim Metrolink manager for TfGM since 2008.

He will take over the post on February 4 – just days before the planned opening of the new Metrolink line to Droylsden.

Mr Cushing said: "I'm delighted and looking forward to the exciting challenges ahead.

"The Metrolink network will soon become the biggest light rail system in the country and, as part of that, is undergoing the most significant change in its history.

"For me, the aim is to continue the fantastic work Philip and his team have done in very challenging circumstances, managing the delivery of the expansion – the largest transport project in the country outside London – at the same time as running an effective day-to-day operation."

Metrolink is undergoing a £1.4bn expansion, with new lines to Ashton-under-Lyne, East Didsbury, Manchester Airport, and through Oldham and Rochdale town centres.

It emerged earlier this month that TfGM is fighting against a claim for £42.3m by its contractor Thales Transport and Security following a series of delays to the opening of new tram lines.

Problems installing a new signalling system delayed lines to Chorlton and Oldham, while extensions to Rochdale and Droylsden are also behind schedule.

Coun Andrew Fender, the chairman of the TfGM Committee, said: "Peter's appointment puts Metrolink in very capable hands.

"He is thought of very highly within the industry and brings a great deal of experience to the role.

"In recent years he has been supporting the existing team while we deliver the £1.4 billion Metrolink expansion."

As we closed for press the Manchester Evening News was reporting the appointment of the new Metrolink boss, Mr Peter Cushing, replacing his former boss Philip Purdy, who is returning to Australia. We look forward to reporting on Mr Cushing's progress in his new role when we produce our next volume in this series, covering the completion of the extension to Rochdale.

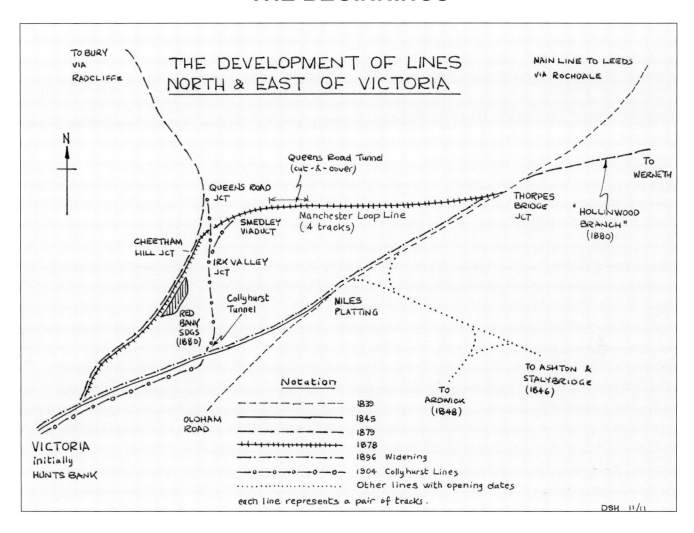

Manphester to Rochdale

The first train arrived at Rochdale from Manchester on Wednesday, 3rd July 1839 when the Manchester and Leeds Railway (MLR) opened its main line as far as Littleborough, pending completion of the Summit Tunnel. The nearest station to Oldham was at Mills Hill. The Manchester terminus was at Oldham Road, so as to avoid the steep descent into Manchester. The complete line through Summit Tunnel to Normanton and Leeds was opened on 1st March, 1841.

Even in those early days Manchester had three terminal stations. The Liverpool and Manchester Railway (LMR) had its terminus at Liverpool Road, opened in 1830. The Manchester & Bolton Railway (MBR) had its terminus on a viaduct at New Bailey Street in Salford, opened in 1838. The MLR station was at Oldham Road and opened in 1839.

The inconvenience of this situation was apparent and a Bill was presented jointly to Parliament to provide a link between the LMR through Salford to meet the

MLR which would be extended down the hill from Miles Platting to Hunts Bank. The Act was passed on 1st July 1839 and included powers to build, inter alia, a branch to Oldham.

The 2.39 mile extension of the line down to Hunts Bank station, shortly to be renamed Victoria, involved gradients of 1 in 47 and 1 in 59. It was inspected by General Pasley on 29th December 1843 and opened on 1st January, 1844. Miles Platting station also opened on the same day. Initially, it was worked by a stationary engine at Miles Platting, but this had ceased by March 1845. With the opening of Hunts Bank/Victoria, Oldham Road ceased to be a passenger station after only 4½ years and thenceforward became the LYR's principal goods depot in the City. An interesting point of social history is that Thomas Edmondson, who invented the machine for printing and date-stamping railway tickets, was the Chief Booking Clerk at Oldham Road.

At the time of its opening Victoria station was the largest railway station in Britain. It was being enlarged continuously and major alterations took place in 1885 and again in 1903. It remained much the same, apart from bomb damage during the Manchester Blitz in 1940/41, until the arrival of Metrolink and the construction of the MEN Arena over the re-aligned north through platforms. Manchester Victoria is dealt with further in the next chapter.

Manchester to Oldham (Werneth)

The 1839 Act provided powers for the MLR to build a line from near Mills Hill to the Werneth District west of Oldham town centre. The branch was surveyed by George Stephenson and Thomas Gooch, both famous names in the development of early railways, in 1840. Gooch estimated the cost of the line at £45,000 and the first contract was let in 1841. The line was inspected by General Pasley and opened to passengers on 31st March 1842. The branch involved the famous 1 in 27 Werneth Incline which was initially worked by a stationary engine. This practice ceased in the mid-1850's.

The branch was an immediate success carrying an average of 750,000 passengers per year for the first few years. At the point where the Oldham Branch left the MLR main line a new station was built and opened on 31st March 1842 and named 'Oldham Junction'. On 11th August 1842 it was renamed 'Middleton' and Mills Hill, formerly the station for Oldham, was closed. In March 1852 'Middleton' became 'Middleton Junction' even though the Middleton branch was not opened until 5th January 1857. Newton Heath station was opened on 1st December 1853.

Werneth to Mumps

Plans to extend the railway from Werneth to Oldham proper were prepared by Thomas Gooch in 1844 and powers were obtained in the MLR Act passed on 30th June 1845. It was originally proposed as a single line, but with the formation of the Oldham Alliance Railway Company (referred to later) works were enlarged to accommodate double tracks. The contract to build the line, including two tunnels, Werneth and Central, was awarded to a Mr George Thomson in October 1845 and the tunnels and permanent way were completed by 6th August 1847. The contract for the terminal station at Mumps was awarded to Coulthard & Foggit on 8th June 1847 and the line from Werneth to Mumps was opened on 1st November 1847. Werneth tunnel, immediately beyond that station, was 471 yards in length. Its completion coincided with the railway company's change of name from the Manchester & Leeds Railway to the Lancashire & Yorkshire Railway on 9th July 1847. The crest of the new company was displayed on the portal of the tunnel on a plinth above the arch. There was then a 200 yard long cutting leading to Central tunnel (449 yards in length). Oldham Central station was just beyond the second tunnel.

The Oldham Railway Alliance

Delays to trains and problems with Werneth incline led to pressure to build a direct route from Manchester Victoria to Werneth. In 1845 there were two rival schemes to build this route; one promoted by the Oldham & District Railway and the other by the grandly-named Oldham, Manchester, Birkenhead & Liverpool Railway. These two parties came together with the MLR to promote a Bill under the title of the Oldham Alliance Railway, to which reference has already been made. Each of the three companies was to provide £150,000 capital. Each company was to pay half their sum, then unite with the MLR. This was achieved early in 1847. This Bill received Royal Assent on 22nd July 1847 and authorised the following lines:

> Oldham Mumps to Ashton-under-Lyne
> Ashton-under-Lyne to Guide Bridge
> Oldham Mumps to Rochdale, including the Royton branch
> Werneth to Miles Platting, including a branch from Hollinwood to Oak Colliery

These were ambitious proposals which unfortunately could not be funded. An Abandonment Act was passed in 1850 before any of the works were undertaken. The lines were subsequently built but not all by the LYR. The Oldham, Ashton & Guide Bridge Railway (OAGBR) was built under an Act passed on 10th August 1857. It opened on 25th August 1861. The line was jointly built and operated by the LNWR and the Manchester, Sheffield and Lincolnshire Railway (MSL). The OAGBR joined the Werneth to Mumps line just north of Oldham Central station. Because its alignment prevented it from using Central the OAGBR built a station at Clegg Street near to the junction which was opened on 1st July 1864. The OAGBR closed to passengers on 4th May 1959. Previously, on 5th July 1856, the LNWR had opened its line between Oldham and Greenfield, so now there were two stations in the Mumps area, one LYR, known as 'Mumps', the other LNWR known as 'Glodwick Road'. Altogether Oldham now had five stations!

Oldham to Rochdale

The Oldham Mumps to Rochdale line was proposed early in 1847 and abandoned in 1850, but the LYR subsequently applied for powers under their Rochdale and Royton Branches Act of 1859. On 29th October 1861 James Gow's tender of £81,317 for construction of formation and track for the 6.56 miles was accepted and William Brown was appointed Resident Engineer on 18th February 1862. Separate contracts were let for stations at Royton, Royton Junction, Shaw, New Hey and Milnrow, and also for goods sheds at Royton, Shaw and Milnrow.

Passenger services started between Oldham and Rochdale on 2nd November 1863 and the Royton Branch was opened on 21st March 1864. Royton Junction station was built in the 'Y' of the junction from Oldham and thus had four platform faces. Later substantial sidings facilities were provided at Royton

Junction. The total cost of the Oldham to Rochdale line was £350,549. The summit of the line, and the highest point between Manchester and Rochdale, is reached at Heyside between Royton Junction and Shaw, where it is 613 feet above sea level.

The Manchester to Oldham direct line

This is sometimes referred to as the Hollinwood Branch. It will be appreciated that whilst Oldham and Rochdale were now linked, there was still no direct link between Manchester and Werneth as originally proposed in 1845, 19 years earlier! An alignment from Thorpes Bridge Junction to Oldham Werneth was re-surveyed and a new estimate prepared on 3rd November 1858.

The estimated cost was £250,000. However, the work was again postponed.

Acts of 1872 and 1873 authorised the construction of lines from Victoria to Radcliffe (for Bury) via Prestwich and Whitefield and for a line from a new junction at Thorpes Bridge to Werneth. The line through to Bury opened on 1st September 1879. To spread the costs the line to Oldham was to be built in two stages, Thorpes Bridge to Hollinwood and Hollinwood to Werneth. The line from Victoria right through to Oldham was opened on 17th May 1880. There were intermediate stations at Dean Lane (2¾ miles from Victoria) and Hollinwood (4¾ miles). Failsworth station (3¼ miles) was opened a year later. In spite of avoiding the Werneth Incline, there was still a difference in level of 255 feet in the 3½ miles from Thorpes Bridge Junction to Werneth station, which involved over half of it having a gradient of 1 in 50.

This photograph of the locomotive "Victoria" is said to have been taken while it was at work on the construction of the Hollinwood branch from Thorpes Bridge to Werneth between 1878 and 1880. "Victoria" was one of four 'Bury-type' locomotives built by the Liverpool firm of Bury, Curtis and Kennedy for the Manchester and Bolton Railway for its opening in 1838. It pulled the first train between Manchester and Bolton on the first day of operation and later passed to the East Lancashire Railway and subsequently to the Lancashire and Yorkshire in 1847. These locomotives were originally 0-4-0s but were rebuilt by the LYR as 0-4-2s by the simple expedient of adding a pair of carrying wheels behind the firebox. In 1878 it was one of a pair sold for £550 each to the contractor working on the Hollinwood branch where it regained it name "Victoria", which had been removed. The LYR bought both the engines back for £200 each on completion of the work in 1880. *(LYRS)*

Number 519 was an Aspinall 2-4-2T of LYR class 5 (later K2) of which 309 were built between 1889 and 1910. Hughes later built another 20 of these engines in 1911 fitted with superheaters as class 6 (later K3) and 44 of the original engines, including 519, were rebuilt to this design. 519 was renumbered 10917 by the LMS in 1923 but did not survive into BR days. *(LYRS)*

Oldham Mumps station with staff in the early 1900s. The down (Rochdale) platform is on the left with the south bay on the right. *(LYRS)*

Milnrow station in 1910 with a LYR 2-4-2T arriving with a Manchester-Rochdale stopping train.

Exterior of Rochdale station in 1913, decorated for the visit of HM King George V to Rochdale. *(LYRS)*

IMPROVEMENTS AND DEVELOPMENTS

Once the line from Thorpes Bridge Junction to Werneth had been opened in May 1880, there were few significant developments to the basic railway route map in the area east of Manchester. There were more-or-less continuous alterations to sidings, loops, junctions, goods and passenger facilities to cope with ever-increasing traffic levels. Some of those relating to our sphere of interest are referred to in this chapter.

Oldham Mumps

Mumps is the name of the thoroughfare from the junction of Yorkshire Street and Union Street, leading to Lees Road and the Bottom o' th' Moor. As we have seen, the first station opened at Mumps on 1st November 1847. With the increasing amount of traffic, and the opening of the direct line from Manchester, reconstruction of the station started in 1884 and was completed in 1887. The station now had a main island platform, with single track bays at each end. The Manchester end was controlled by Mumps No 2 Signal Box and the Rochdale end by Mumps No 3 Signal Box. The island platform was approached by a subway from the town. In 1957 the old station frontage was knocked down and replaced by a modern one-storey brick structure. Electric lighting was installed throughout the station at this time. The Rochdale bay was taken out-of-use in May 1967. The period 1968/69 saw the construction of the Oldham byass on the A62, which required the demolition of some existing railway bridges and their reconstruction as well as the building of new ones.

Rochdale Station

The original Rochdale station opened in 1839 and was located a little further east than the later (and current) railway station. It was adjacent to Moss Lane and accessed from Milnrow Road. The opening of the line from Oldham in 1863, and the construction of the Bacup branch in 1870, added to the growing pressures on the original station. A tender to build a new station, and to widen the approach from the west, was advertised in January 1886. Due to problems with the contractor the station did not open fully until January 1892. The new station consisted of two substantial island platforms, one lying between the down pair of tracks and the other between the up pair. The down platform had a double-track bay for services departing towards Bacup, Todmorden or Oldham. The up platform also had a double track bay for services departing southwards towards Manchester via Castleton or to Bolton via Bury and westwards to the coast.

Travelling towards Rochdale from Manchester the first signal box on the widened approach was Castleton Sidings followed by Rochdale West. Beyond the station there were signal boxes at Rochdale Goods Yard and Rochdale East Junction, where the Oldham branch left the main line. This box controlled the junctions for both the Oldham and Bacup branches. There was also a Rochdale Branch Sidings signal box at the start of the Bacup branch controlling the exchange and marshalling sidings on the down side, including an extensive coal yard. Sometime between 1953 and 1965 the station clock tower was removed. Nevertheless, the station continued to have a more impressive appearance than its opposite number at Oldham Mumps.

The Bacup Branch

The branch from Rochdale up the Whitworth Valley was opened to Facit in 1870 and extended to Bacup in 1881. This was the 'mountain line' of the LYR and with a summit at Britannia 967 ft above sea level and gradients as steep as 1 in 34 it was always a difficult line to work. Passenger use had declined severely over the years as a consequence of stiff competition from frequent Rochdale Corporation electric trams and then buses on the adjacent road. A coal shortage following a severe winter gave the LMS a convenient excuse to discontinue the passenger service 'temporarily' on 16th June 1947 and this withdrawal was formalised by BR in 1949. The line was then closed sequentially to all other traffic: from Facit to Bacup Engine Shed in 1952, through to Bacup in 1954 and from Facit to Whitworth in 1963, followed by complete closure on 19th August 1967.

Manchester Victoria and its easterly approaches

When the station opened in 1844, Victoria station consisted of one long platform, with a single bay at each end. As traffic increased, particularly from the east and north as branches were developed, the station was successively enlarged. The first enlargement was in 1855, when a separate suburban station, with bay platforms, was opened, known originally as Ducie Bridge, to handle services from Oldham, Middleton and Ashton. In 1865 additional platforms were built north of the station, adjacent to New Bridge Street, to accommodate Bolton line trains. In 1877, following removal of some earlier works, five east-facing bays were opened. With the withdrawal of all LNW traffic in June 1884, on the opening of its own station at Exchange, the LYR carried out another major re-organisation. By this time the station had 13 platform faces.

Increasing traffic and the steep gradients of the two track main line from Victoria to Miles Platting Junction led to the proposal to build a four track railway from the east end of Victoria station to Thorpes Bridge via

Smedley Junction about 1925 showing the 4-track Manchester Loop, the chord line to Irk Valley Junction and the Collyhurst Viaduct carrying the Bury line across the valley and the loop. Metrolink will come down the chord line and then follow the loop line towards the photographer. A new access to Queens Road depot has been built to the right of the picture. *(BCL)*

Cheetham Hill and Red Bank. This was known as the Manchester Loop line and opened on 1st August 1878. Despite the relief given by the Manchester Loop line, the LYR took Powers in 1890 and 1891 to widen the original line from Victoria to Miles Platting and Thorpes Bridge Junction. Additional carriage sidings, with a capacity of 66 coaches, were also provided at Red Bank in 1890. The pairs of tracks on the widening were designated Fast and Slow and gave access to the east-facing bays built in 1877. It has to be remembered that all the works to the east and south of the original Victoria station required major civil engineering work to bridge over the River Irk and several reconstructions of what we now call Cheetham Hill Road Bridge. The widening works had to be phased so as not to interfere with railway operation and were brought into use on 6th June 1905.

The Collyhurst Lines

The LYR promoted an Act in 1895 to enable it to construct what are known as the Collyhurst Lines to enable trains from Bury via Whitefield and Prestwich to reach the east-facing bay platforms on the south side of Victoria station, adjacent to Corporation Street. This was much more convenient for city commuters than using the bay platform on the north side of the station. With the increasing competition from the recently-electrified tramways, this became a major issue. To do this it was necessary to construct a link from Queens Road Junction on the Cheetham Hill–Bury line across the Irk Valley to Collyhurst. This required the construction of iron spans over the Manchester Loop lines, a 5-arched brick viaduct across the Irk Valley and a 115 foot skew bow lattice span across Collyhurst Road. A connecting chord line, also on a brick-arched viaduct, was built from between the Collyhurst Road bridge and Irk Valley Viaduct to Smedley Viaduct on the Loop lines. This series of bridges led into Collyhurst Tunnel (426 yards) to emerge on the south side of the approach tracks to Victoria and so into the bay platforms. It was brought into use on 3rd October 1904. By this time the station had 17 platforms and covered 13½ acres.

From then on, apart from the electrification of the Holcombe Brook-Bury-Victoria service in April 1916, there were no further significant changes to Victoria station. The final and full extent of the approaches to Victoria and the track layout and principle features are shown on the next page. However, the station was badly bombed in 1940. Initially, platforms 1 to 3

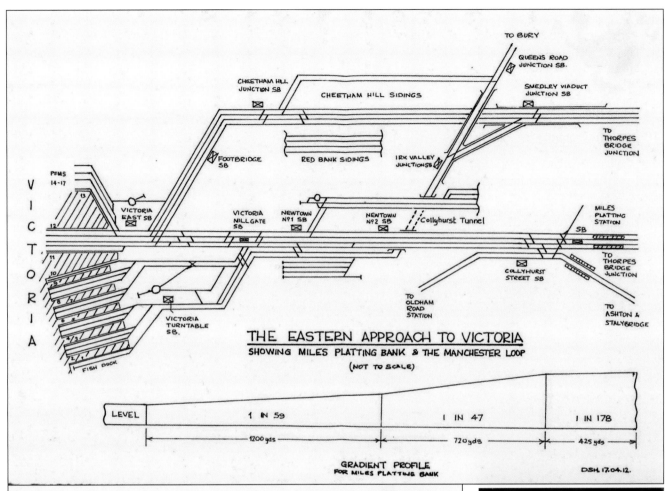

THE EASTERN APPROACH TO VICTORIA

SHOWING MILES PLATTING BANK & THE MANCHESTER LOOP

(NOT TO SCALE)

LEVEL	1 IN 59	1 IN 47	1 IN 178
	1200 yds	720 yds	425 yds

GRADIENT PROFILE
FOR MILES PLATTING BANK

DSH. 17.04.12.

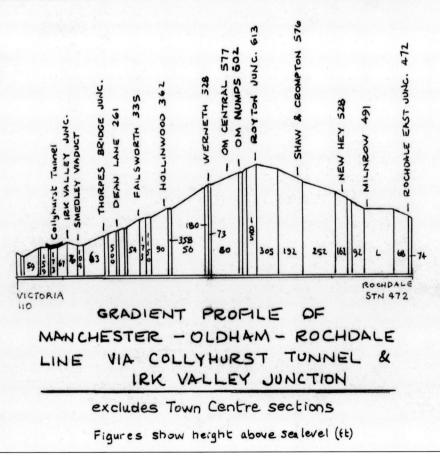

GRADIENT PROFILE OF
MANCHESTER – OLDHAM – ROCHDALE
LINE VIA COLLYHURST TUNNEL &
IRK VALLEY JUNCTION

excludes Town Centre sections

Figures show height above sea level (ft)

were equipped with third-rail but subsequently this was transferred to platforms 4 and 5 and platforms 1 to 3 were taken out of use by the early 1970's. The Beeching Report in the mid 1960's had proposed the withdrawal of many East Lancashire suburban services, including the Bury electric line. Exchange Station closed on 5th May 1969 with services being transferred to Victoria.

The Blackley Branch

The 1899 Act, which authorised the widening of the railway to accommodate the south end of the Collyhurst line, also authorised the construction of a new railway from the Manchester Loop, through Blackley, to join end-on with the Middleton Branch. The line would have been 4.96 miles in length and would have left the Loop line immediately west of Queens Road tunnel. It would have served Harpurhey, Blackley and Alkrington and provided a more direct service to Middleton. However, as the local electric tramways were already making big inroads to the receipts of LYR suburban services, the company decided to apply for abandonment powers that were granted in 1904. It is of interest to note that 60 years later the Manchester Rapid Transit Study proposed a similar line.

Wartime Bombing

On the night of 22nd December 1940 Exchange Station suffered serious bomb damage. The following night it was the turn of Victoria Station to suffer serious damage. This second attack also took out the Control Room and the Emergency Control Room, thus hindering rail operations over a wide area of the north-west. It is fair to say that the overall roof at Victoria never fully recovered from this bombing.

Electrification

In 1882 a branch 3¾ miles long had been built from Bury to Holcome Brook. To compete with the electric trams, additional halts were opened and a steam rail motor was introduced in 1905. At the initiative of Dick, Kerr and Company (well-known in the electric traction field and a constituent of English Electric) who were bidding for an electrification project in South America, the branch was electrified on the 3500v dc overhead system and two units (powered car plus trailer) were built. The electric service started in 1913.

Work started on the Manchester Victoria–Bury electrification in 1914 when the line was converted to

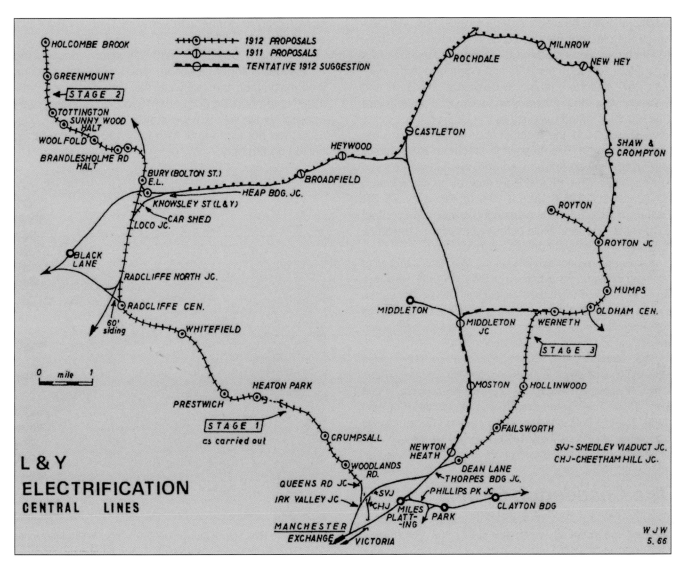

15

electric traction and opened in April, 1916. This used the 1200v dcside contact system which was different to both the original Holcombe Brook and Liverpool–Southport electrification schemes. Initially, this was four-rail return-current (as with London Underground) but eventually the fourth rail was dispensed with. The unique Bury–Holcombe Brook section was converted to 1200v dc operation and through third-rail services operated from March 1918. The normal make-up was a five-car train of which three cars were powered. Wartime emergencies, post-war controls and the amalgamation with the LNW ensured delays to any further ideas of electrification.

However, in 1924 the newly-formed London Midland & Scottish Railway (LMS) considered electrifying from Victoria to Oldham and Shaw, including the Royton branch: 12 route miles on the 1200v dc system. There were to have been improvements at Oldham Mumps, Werneth and Shaw and electrification of sidings at Newton Heath. The proposed routing was to follow the Bury line as far as Irk Valley Junction and then take the chord line to Smedley Viaduct thus avoiding the complications at Miles Platting. There was to have been a basic 20 minute service to Shaw and Royton, with additional trains between Victoria and Mumps. At a later stage the electrification could be continued from Shaw to Rochdale as well as the direct line to Rochdale via Castleton. Although the Bury line continued to flourish, with new stations opening at Besses o' the Barn and Bowker Vale, the Oldham/Shaw/Royton plans were never implemented because of the Depression.

In March 1951 the electrification equipment on the Bury–Holcombe Brook section became life-expired. Steam trains were introduced until the line was closed in May 1952. The original Bury line rolling stock lasted 43 years until 1959 when it was replaced by 26 BR Standard 2-car EMUs fitted with the unique side contact third-rail equipment. Most of these lasted until the line's closure for Metrolink conversion in 1991.

Regular passenger services on the Middleton Junction to Werneth section were withdrawn on 9th June 1958. However, an early morning Rochdale–Manchester DMU continued to use the line until 5th January 1963. It continued to be used as a diversionary route on Sundays in April and May 1960, when the Hollinwood line was re-ballasted.

The Oldham Clegg Street-Delph service (The Delph Donkey) was taken off in 1955 and the Oldham, Ashton and Guide Bridge line (OAGB) was closed to passengers on 2nd May, 1959. The Royton branch was closed on 16th April 1966. The line from Chadderton Junction to Werneth closed completely on 7th January 1963, followed by the Oldham-Greenfield branch in 1964. Oldham Central was closed on 18th April, 1966.

The Chadderton Branch

Chadderton Junction, at the foot of the 1 in 27 incline, marked the point at which the 0.87 mile freight-only Chadderton branch diverted from the Werneth line. The Chadderton Goods line was opened as late as 1914 and ran to a goods and coal yard adjacent to Hunt Lane. It remained in use as a rail-served coal depot until the late 1980's, after which Middleton Junction West signal box was closed and Middleton Junction was a junction no more.

Services on the Middleton branch had been steadily reduced, so that by 1960 there was a peak-hour only service on weekdays of five trains each way. These ceased on 7th September 1961, and the line closed completely in 1966.

With the closure of the Middleton Branch the chord line from Irk Valley Junction to Smedley Viaduct was no longer required and was closed completely on 7th February 1966. Oldham Parcels Concentration Depot on the site of the former Clegg Street Goods Yard was opened in 1960. Between 7th and 21st May 1967 major track-work and signalling alterations took place in the Oldham area. On 21st May six signal boxes – Sheepwashers Lane, Waterloo Sidings, Werneth Station and Mumps Nos. 1, 2 & 3 were closed and replaced by a new box at Oldham Mumps. In 1968/69 substantial bridgeworks took place in the Mumps area as a consequence of the new road layout being constructed in connection with the Oldham By-Pass, which opened on 6th October 1970.

On 28th October 1980 flooding closed the Hollinwood–Oldham section, but single-line working was introduced the following day and continued until 13th November. On 30th April 1985 Derker station was opened. However, Royton station (it lost 'Junction' in 1978) did not close until 11th May 1987, the last train calling on 8th May.

On 4th June 1958 Stanier Black Five 4-6-0 number 44895 approaches New Hey with the 17.06 Victoria to Rochdale. *(BH)*

Werneth to Mumps

Above: Werneth Junction from the up platform of Oldham Werneth Station. The original line goes straight on down the Werneth incline, while the Hollinwood loop goes off to the left, running parallel to the original line before curving off to the left. Note the Midland / LMS-style signal box. Featherstall Road bridge crosses the junction in front of Platts Mill. The footbridge on the right connects the down platform with Featherstall Road. *(MLS)*

Below: Werneth Junction from the Manchester end with the direct line from Thorpes Bridge Junction, the Hollinwood branch, coming in from the right. The 1 in 27 gradient can be seen rising up into the station platforms, beyond which can be seen Werneth tunnel The elevated walkway leading from Featherstall Road to the station platforms is on the left. *(RSG)*

Above: A cast iron girder made by R Ormerod and Son of Manchester in 1842 supported Featherstall Road where it crossed the former goods line alongside Platts Mill. *(RSG)*

Above: Oldham Central station c1925 looking towards Mumps with a Manchester-bound commuter train arriving. *(PHC)*

Below: The new Oldham Mumps signal box built to the BR standard design for a mechanical box. Beyond is the LYR-design Waterloo Sidings signal box which it was about to replace. This box was one of six replaced by the new box on 21st May 1967.

Left: A detail of the Manchester end of the down platform showing the BR London Midland Region-style name sign, the gradient post indicator at the top of the Werneth incline and the steps leading up to the footbridge to Featherstall Road. *(MLS)*

STEAM OPERATION

Traffic Patterns

The Manchester Victoria-Oldham-Rochdale line was built to serve the ever-increasing needs of those expanding cotton towns and their intermediate communities, such as Hollinwood and Royton and to link these towns to Manchester - the centre of the cotton world. Over the years an intensive passenger train service developed for both business and pleasure purposes. A feature of passenger operations was the provision of excursion trains in connection with Wakes Weeks (Mill Holidays) and special events like the Grand National.

There was also heavy freight traffic of cotton and coal inwards and returning empties outwards, as well as extensive general merchandise traffic. With the development of tramways and their electrification in the 1900s, the competition for local passengers became intense. General merchandise traffic started to suffer from road competition in the 1920s and 1930s. With the growth of mail order business after World War 2, there came a substantial parcels business. The coal and cotton business continued until the demise of the cotton trade from the 1960s.

The line was very steeply graded, particularly the section from Thorpes Bridge to Royton, and this often meant the double-heading of the excursion trains and the division of freight trains into smaller sections at Royton Junction Sidings.

Following the completion of the direct line from Thorpes Bridge Junction to Werneth and on to Oldham and Rochdale in 1880, the trains operated from the bay platforms then numbered 1- 5 at Victoria, going directly up the bank and past Miles Platting. After the opening of the Collyhurst Line in 1904 and the rebuilding of Victoria Station, trains to Oldham-Royton-Rochdale, Middleton, Bury and Bacup operated out of the east-facing bays numbered 1 - 10. Trains for Oldham, Royton, Rochdale and Middleton had the alternative of continuing on the original route via Miles Platting or taking the new route through Collyhurst tunnel as far as Irk Valley Junction, then following the spur – all on viaduct - to Smedley Viaduct where they joined the Manchester Loop, continuing their journey to Thorpes Bridge Junction. This situation continued until the withdrawal of some local services in the 1960. Platforms 1 – 3 were equipped with the third rail for the Bury line services of 3-trains-per-hour, which opened throughout in 1916. In LMS days the Bury electric line service offered 6 trains per hour in the afternoons, rising to 10 in the evening peak. Seven trains could leave Victoria at the same time, five to the east and two to the west. The greatest number scheduled to leave in the 20th century were five at 5.10 p.m. (17.10), when there were departures to Blackpool, Atherton, York, Middleton and Prestwich.

Timetables

The July 1922 timetable shows 11 trains in the morning peak from Mumps to Victoria, five having come from Rochdale, five from Royton and one from Shaw & Crompton. The evening peak service from Victoria showed seven trains to Mumps; four continuing to Royton and three to Rochdale. Off-peak there were 18 trains in the Up between Mumps and Victoria and 19 in the Down direction. Four trains came from Rochdale (five to Rochdale) and eight from Royton (six to Royton) in the off-peak. Journey times were 45 - 48 minutes from Rochdale via Mumps and 32 to/from Royton. Trains from Mumps to Manchester typically took 22 minutes, with those going up the grade from Manchester taking 25 minutes. In the later 1920s and early 1930s there were still 48 trains each way per day between Victoria and Mumps.

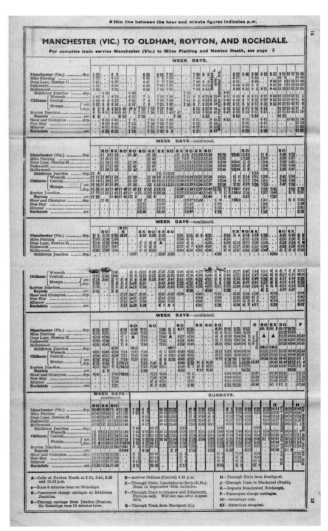

The 1938 timetable for the Oldham Loop line.

18

These two scale models of an Aspinall 2-4-2T and an Attock coach show better than anything else the locomotives and rolling stock which were the mainstay of the Oldham Loop for so many years.

Motive Power

For much of the line's life the Aspinall 2-4-2 tanks provided the power for the passenger services on the line. These locos, of which there was a total of 330 built over a period from 1889 to 1911, provided the main motive power for the L & Y suburban services throughout the system. In 1910 for a short period they were supplanted by Hoy's 2-6-2T development, designed especially for the heavily graded lines such as Victoria-Oldham-Rochdale. However, these 20 locomotives were not successful and they were quietly retired to other duties from 1913. Once more the Aspinall 2-4-2T's reigned supreme, well into the LMS years, past the Grouping of the railways in 1923. In the 1930s the Aspinall 2-4-2T locos were still handling the Victoria-

Oldham-Royton-Rochdale trains, although they were augmented by Fowler 2-6-2 tanks, and later by Stanier 2-6-4 tanks. There were still 81 Aspinall tanks in traffic in 1951, and then followed Fairburn 2-6-4Ts and BR Standard Class 4 tanks of the 80000 series.

Of course, the line was host to a great variety of larger locomotives required to handle the Wakes Weeks trains and excursions to Aintree for the Grand National and Illuminations Specials to Blackpool, Morecambe and North Wales. Black 5s and Horwich 'Crabs' would appear regularly on the scene, as well as Fowler 4F 0-6-0s, and suchlike. Occasionally a 'Patriot' or 'Jubilee' 4-6-0 would appear on the specials and empty stock workings. In later years BR Standard Class 5 4-6-0s and Britannia Pacifics were observed occasionally. At these times there was also frequent double-heading involving many interesting combinations of locomotives, often mixing the generations. It was not unusual to see a forty year old Aspinall 0-6-0 of Lancashire & Yorkshire origin piloting a Black 5 or even a Standard 5.

Coaching Stock

For most of the period rakes of three or four non-corridor coaches provided services and offered all three classes of accommodation. The L & Y were one of the last railways to give up three-class accommodation, reluctantly doing so on 1st January 1912 – 49 years after the Midland Railway had taken the lead and 26 years after the Great Northern had removed second class! Train lengths would usually double for peak periods.

Initially, 3-axle coaches were used, replaced in the late 1880s by bogied coaches. In 1904 the L&Y introduced Attock-designed four-coach trains of six-a-side compartment stock with an empty weight of 100 tons. These trains would be able to carry between 400 & 450 passengers. In due course non-corridor LMS sets of more modern design were introduced. The final sets were of BR Standard non-corridor stock. Excursion trains were often made up of similar stock (despite the lack of toilet accommodation), but in later years modern corridor stock of the period would sometimes be provided. From the early part of the 20th century there was a direct service operated by the LNWR from Rochdale via Oldham and Stockport to London Euston. For the June Wakes Week in 1955, 15 additional trains were run on Friday night/Saturday morning to the usual north west coast resorts, but also to Bournemouth, the West of England and East Coast resorts.

A Rochdale to Manchester local passes Heyside in the country section between Shaw and Royton Junction behind Stanier 2-6-4T number 42486. *(PH)*

The Irk Valley accident

On the steeply graded lines between Manchester, Oldham and Rochdale there were, over the years, a number of accidents. Many of these involved unbraked freight trains running away, but on Saturday 15th August 1953 there was a serious accident at Irk Valley Junction where the spur from the Bury line went down to Smedley Viaduct. At that time the junction was controlled by a 20-lever signal box standing on the Down side of the line, overlooking the junction. There were home and distant signals protecting the junction, but there were no track circuits and no block controls on any of the signals.

The accident occurred on the junction itself, when the 07.20 electric service from Bury to Victoria hit the steam locomotive (a 2-6-4 tank) of the four-coach 07.36 from Victoria to Bacup, a glancing blow. Unfortunately, the front coach of the electric train cannoned off the locomotive and went over the edge of the viaduct into the valley below. Nine passengers and the driver of the electric train (a former Mayor of Bury) were killed and 24 passengers badly injured. Had the accident occurred on a weekday the consequences would have been much worse.

The reasons for the accident were, as usual, complex, but the official inquiry revealed a number of serious signal deficiencies and an unsatisfactory level of supervision. At the time there was a chronic staff shortage and it was difficult to recruit suitable staff. Nevertheless, the accident sent serious shock waves throughout the railway industry.

Freight and Parcels

There was a considerable amount of freight activity on the line with coal and cotton to the multitude of mills en route, and the associated return working of empty wagons. There was also a lot of general merchandise traffic well into the 1960s. Coal trains came mainly from the Yorkshire pits via the Calder Valley line to Rochdale, where they would reverse and go forward direct to their destinations, or the Royton sidings for sorting down for local trip-working to their final destination. Empties would be accumulated at Royton for return to Yorkshire via Rochdale. Parcels both inwards and outwards became an increasingly important traffic, particularly with the growth in mail order catalogues. A Parcels Concentration Depot was built at Oldham in 1960. Much of the freight was handled by Fowler 7F 0-8-0s or by Stanier & WD 2-8-0s. Cravens also built three Diesel Parcels Vans that were used on the line in the 1960s.

Following the Beeching proposals local goods yards began to close in the mid 1960s. Freight trains were removed from the Oldham-Rochdale section in August 1967, followed by the withdrawal of parcels trains a month later. Certain of these were still steam-worked.

On a sunny July evening in 1958 a Rochdale-bound commuter train leaves Shaw and Crompton, unusually powered by Fowler class 4F 0-6-0 number 44543. The Briar Mill in the background beyond the station is still in use as a trading estate, but everything else in the picture has gone. *(PH)*

The WD class 'Austerity' 2-8-0s were a common sight on the main line through Castleton, but seldom ventured around the loop. In June 1955 number 90388 waits for the road at Royton Junction with an Oldham to Moston transfer freight train. *(PH)*

DIESELISATION

Early conversions

In the early 1950's BR was considering introducing Diesel Multiple Units (DMUs) onto local passenger services. Five trial areas had been identified: Leeds/ Bradford, East Anglia, Lincolnshire, West Cumberland and Newcastle. The Leeds/Bradford scheme commenced on 14th June 1954 with eight 2-car Derby lightweight DMUs. They were an immediate success with substantially increased passenger levels and reductions in operating costs. BR had 70 DMUs in 1954, 179 in 1955 and 453 by 1956. The Modernisation Plan of 1955 then kicked into effect and in 1957 there were 1,349 DMUs. The DMU fleet was ultimately to grow to over 4,000 units before the Beeching cuts took effect.

The Manchester-Oldham-Royton/Rochdale local services were gradually turned over to diesel operation as part of the North Manchester Dieselisation scheme in February 1958. Two-car units, operated as four-car trains in the peak, provided the services. Each power car had two, 150hp AEC or Leyland engines (more latterly, BUT after they combined their resources). Because of the gradients involved in the area both cars of a two-car unit were powered, giving a total horsepower of 600. Services were accelerated and often put on an even-interval basis. Two-car DMUs built by Cravens of Sheffield were based on the new Diesel Maintenance Depot at Newton Heath. Services on the main line direct from Victoria to Rochdale had to await the Dieselisation of the Calder Valley services, which came in 1962.

Cravens of Sheffield were one of seven private rolling stock builders who built DMUs under the 1955 Railway Modernisation Plan, in addition to those built by BR themselves. Cravens, who built 405 units, were unusual in adapting the Standard BR Mk I coach profile for their vehicles, to which they fitted a two-windowed cab. Two classes of Cravens-built units served the North Manchester area: Class 105 power trains with AEC or Leyland engines and Class 112 powered twins, each car of which had one Rolls-Royce 238 HP engine.

The transition from steam to diesel begins. On 17th July 1961 a Newton Heath-based Cravens / BUT unit stands in the north bay at Rochdale ready to depart for Manchester via Oldham. In the foreground ex-Midland 4F 0-6-0 number 43734 waits to leave with a Rochdale-Stoke parcels train, an unusual choice of motive power. *(IGH)*

In January 1966 a Birmingham Railway and Carriage Company-built 2-car DMU runs into Milnrow on a Rochdale-Oldham-Manchester working. These units were used to augment the original Cravens-units. *(IGH)*

The Royton Accident

On 8th February 1961, a 2-car Class 112 Cravens DMU ran away down the 1 in 62 gradient from Royton Junction to Royton. Fortunately, it was empty stock with driver and guard only. It had worked a train from Victoria via Oldham to Shaw and was returning empty to Royton to operate the first train to Manchester. The driver jumped out as the train ran through Royton Station at nearly 40 mph. It continued through the buffer stops, demolished a stone wall and dropped several feet onto the road, before coming to rest in a row of terraced houses. The elderly occupants were still in bed when the accident happened and, uninjured, were carried along the roof of the DMU to safety! Recovery was put in hand immediately and normal services were restored at 20.55. The Royton branch closed on 16th April 1966, but Royton Junction retained its name until 1978 when it was renamed 'Royton'.

A Modernisation Plan diesel, a Metro-Cammell two-car class 105/106 unit, approaches Oldham Central on a Royton-Manchester Victoria service in the late 1950s. *(JD)*

A Derby-built unit , incorporating a 4-digit headcode box, enters Shaw and Crompton station on a Rochdale-bound service in 1966. *(PH)*

Operation

The Craven-built DMUs were described as "rattling themselves to bits". They also had a propensity to catch fire and were not popular. They were amongst the earliest withdrawals of DMUs following the Beeching closures. Locally, they were replaced by a mix of Derby Class 108 - or BRCW Class 104 - built DMUs. Occasionally, Calder Valley Class 110 3-car sets would be seen working some services. These were the last BRCW-built sets, had Rolls-Royce 180 hp engines and were amongst the best DMUs built. Of the 30 Class 110 sets built, 10 were originally allocated to the London Midland Region at Newton Heath and it was these sets that found their way on to the Oldham services.

The diesel-operated winter weekday timetable of 1963/64 offered a 20-minute interval service between Victoria and Mumps with alternate trains running to or from Rochdale or Royton. Peak period services provided five trains from Rochdale in the morning, six from Royton and 14 from Mumps. In the evening peak there were five, four and seven trains respectively. In the Down (to Oldham/Rochdale) direction there were five trains to Rochdale in the morning peak (six in the evening peak); four to Royton in both peaks and 11 to Mumps (nine in the evening). The direct (main) line from Victoria to Rochdale had five or six trains per direction per hour in the peak, some of which were to/from Leeds/Bradford and Liverpool. In 1972, when the PTE became responsible for services, there were half-hourly services from Victoria to Mumps, with one an hour going forward to Rochdale. There were two additional trains each way during peak periods.

In May 1979 the condition of the Newton Heath-based DMUs was such that they had to be replaced by local-hauled coaches from the London area. The following year, on 28th June 1980, a 12-car train of DMUs (the longest possible) operated a Wakes Special to and from Llandudno.

Second Generation DMUs

Following withdrawal of Modernisation Plan DMUs, the mainstay of the lines' services was provided by Class 142 'Pacer' units. These were basically Leyland National bus bodies mounted on a 4-wheeler freight wagon chassis. The first unit to operate on the Oldham Loop was 142.007 on 30th September 1985. Other second-generation bogie DMUs providing services were Class 150 'Sprinters' and 'Super Sprinters' of both Classes 155 and 156. All these classes were capable of working in multiples together, unlike the first generation units.

The class 150's were 20m long units with sliding doors at the third-points. Each had a Cummins engine of 285 hp, driving both wheels of the inner bogie. They were built by British Rail Engineering Ltd (BREL) at Derby. Both Classes, 155 and 156, were 23m long with single sliding doors at the ends. Both used the same Cummins engine with the same drive arrangement and bogies. The Class 155 was designed and built by Leyland, using Leyland National bus body parts, at Workington, whilst the Class 156 was designed and built by Metro-Cammell at Birmingham. Body shells for the 156s were built by a number of sub-contractors, including a batch from Standard Wagon at Heywood.

Door problems and a national shortage of suitable trains for lightly-used services led to the conversion of most of the Cass 155s into single-car units designated Class 153. The conversion was done by Hunslet-Barclay at Kilmarnock. These units also saw service on the Oldham Loop, both singly and in multiples. The seven Class 155s owned by West Yorkshire PTE (Metro) remained unaltered and have provided the mainstay of the Leeds-Bradford-Manchester 'Calder Valley' services, and still do to this day! These arrangements, with the units in a variety of liveries, continued until the closure of train services on the Oldham branch on 3rd October 2009. Prior to this a Public Inquiry had been held into the closure of the heavy rail line in preparation for its conversion to Metrolink.

Sectorisation

On the Sectorisation of British Rail, local train services became part of the Provincial Services Sector. Subsequently, in 1979, this was renamed Regional Railways, with separate organisations for the North West and North East. Following the opening of the Windsor Link (between Ordsall Lane and the former Lancashire & Yorkshire line to Bolton/Wigan) and the construction of the new station at Salford Crescent in May 1989, there was a wholesale recasting of local rail services.

With the May timetable of 1990 came the concept of Network North West (modelled on the highly successful Network South East). Inter-alia this led to some off-peak services from Rochdale to Oldham and Manchester Victoria being extended to Blackpool or Southport, in an attempt to generate off-peak traffic. From May to September 1990 there were three local-hauled services using Class 31 or 37 diesels, hauling a motley collection of coaches. On the occasion of a DMU fitter's strike at Newton Heath, loco-hauled trains were used in place of DMUs, which could not be serviced. On at least one occasion a Type 4 Peak Class loco was used!

Beeching and after

In 1963 The Beeching Report on the Reshaping of British Railways had proposed wholesale withdrawal of local passenger services and closure of stations across the BR network. Often the lines in question had recently been dieselised with the consequent improvement to their finances through greatly reduced working costs and increased revenue through their frequent and modern services.

So far as this story goes Beeching proposed the complete withdrawal of the following services and the closure of the intermediate stations served:

Manchester Victoria-Moston–Middleton
Manchester Victoria-Bury Bolton Street
Royton-Royton Junction

The Report also proposed the following services for modification:

Manchester Victoria-Rochdale–Todmorden
Manchester Victoria–Oldham–Rochdale
Bolton – Bury (Knowsley Street)–Rochdale

There were, of course, closure procedures to go through. This led to formal public hearings and, usually, much active protest about the closures. Both the Middleton and Royton branches, and their associated services, were withdrawn in 1966. The Bury electric service survived, but Bolton Street Station lost its through services from Manchester Victoria to Bacup, Accrington and Colne at the end of 1966. The Bolton - Bury (Knowsley Street) - Rochdale service went four years later. As we shall see in the next chapter, both the direct service to Rochdale and the Oldham-Rochdale survived.

However, there then started a continuous programme of attrition, spread over the next 20 years. It appeared as though BR did not want to run the railway and only did so with a bad grace, which affected staff morale and physical assets very badly. The Royton branch closed on 16th April 1966, followed by the closure of Oldham Central on the 18th. All stations on the line were de-staffed from 8th September 1969, although reduced booking office facilities were retained at Mumps. Higginshaw Gas Siding was closed on 6th April 1970, reducing further the freight activity on the line.

In 1973 the station buildings at Shaw & Crompton were demolished. On 6th April the following year, the station was renamed 'Shaw' only to revert to its full title in September 1990. In 1978 Royton Junction became plain 'Royton', although the branch and junction had disappeared 18 years previously. In May 1976 BR proposed the closure of the Shaw-Rochdale section, but GMPTE refused to allow it and paid an increased subsidy for its continued operation. Clegg Street Parcels Depot closed on 1st June 1981 after a 21 year life. A new station was opened at Derker on 30th September 1985.

Signalling

The signal boxes that used to control the line are listed in Appendix 'C'. The whole of the Victoria complex and the Oldham-Rochdale line was controlled by mechanical signalling and Absolute Block Working. Because of the complexity of the track layouts and the closeness of junctions, in places the signal boxes were literally within shouting distance of each other. Some of the boxes were amongst the largest in Britain, staffed continuously by several signalmen, and signal boys being employed to record movements. With completion of works in 1904/5, Victoria East Junction signal box controlled the mainlines (Manchester Loop and up the bank to Miles Platting), whilst Turntable signal box controlled the suburban traffic from the ten bay platforms. Some rationalisation took place in 1884 with the opening of Exchange Station, thus improving the movement of LNW trains through Victoria.

In March 1929 the West end of Victoria was re-signalled with two new all-electric boxes at Deal Street and Victoria West and colour light signalling. This lead to the closure of six old mechanical boxes at Salford LNW, Exchange No. 2 Exchange No.1 Deal Street, Irwell Bridge and Victoria West Junction. The new signalling at the west end of Victoria was a great success, improving operations considerably, and particularly in fog, which was a frequent occurrence. In spite of this the Depression of the 1930s, and the onset of another war precluded any similar improvements to signalling at the east end of the station. However, in the late 1950s work was put in hand to build a new power signal box at Victoria East, located immediately behind the old mechanical box. Some track rationalisation and simplification took place, including interfaces with the west of the station. The new box came into operation on 2nd April 1962 and replaced 6 old boxes: Victoria East Junction, Turntable, Millgate, Newtown No. 1 Newtown No 2 and Footbridge.

On the Oldham - Rochdale line itself Milnrow Signal Box closed on the 11th October 1964, followed by the closure of New Hey on 19th October 1967. On 21st May 1967 a new signal box was commissioned at Mumps, leading to the closure of six older boxes. On 6th July 1980, the line was singled between Shaw and Rochdale East Junction and the level crossing gates at Shaw were replaced by lifting barriers. On 26th June 1994 Hollinwood Signal Box was closed.

To make way for the new Metrolink tracks and the flyover bridge, Rochdale East Junction was closed and removed in 2011. A new Rochdale West Box opened at Castleton on 30th August, 2011. Colour light signals replaced the last remaining semaphore signals in the area.

On a wet May day in 1967 a later version of the Cravens 2-car DMU, each powered by a single Rolls Royce engine, approaches Oldham Mumps. The new signal box is under construction and the gasworks is still much in evidence. These units were based on Accrington for the East Lancashire services but this one had strayed on to the Victoria to Rochdale line. *(IGH)*

In more picturesque surroundings a Derby-built unit stands at New Hey in August 1968 on a Rochdale to Manchester trip with St Thomas's church overseeing proceedings. *(IGH)*

22nd February 1979 was another miserable winter day which coincided with a shortage of diesel units at Newton Heath. Derby-built type 2 locomotive number 25199 and a set of four main line coaches have been pressed into service to cover. *(RSG)*

During the Network North West era of 1990 there were three loco-hauled trains a day each way over the line to and from Blackpool. Most trains were hauled by Brush class 31s but in this view a Railfreight liveried Sulzer class 47 is in charge of an afternoon up train at Heyside between Shaw and Royton. *(RSG)*

On 18th November 1987 Sprinter number 150251 departs from Milnrow on a Victoria-bound service. The track was singled between Shaw and Rochdale in July 1980 as an economy measure. These units could work in multiple with Pacers and other Sprinters.

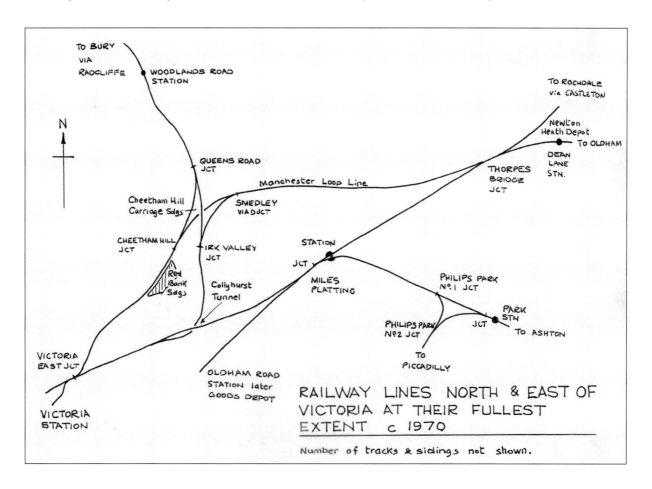

RAILWAY LINES NORTH & EAST OF VICTORIA AT THEIR FULLEST EXTENT c 1970

Number of tracks & sidings not shown.

SURVIVAL

One of the reasons for establishing the Passenger Transport Executives (PTEs) in 1969 was for them to produce transport plans that would integrate bus and train services. As a step towards this, PTE's were expected to take financial responsibility for those local rail services, the implications being that if they did not do so those services would be withdrawn. In November 1969 when the South-East Lancashire and North-East Cheshire (SELNEC) PTE was set up there were 25 rail services operating, of which seven were internal to the SELNEC area. The remaining 18 were cross-boundary. PTE's had to have regard to places 25 miles beyond their boundary and there was a location near Crewe that could be influenced by three PTEs! Of these services, five were already slated for closure under the Beeching Plan. They were:

    Romiley-Macclesfield
    New Mills-Hayfield
    Rochdale-Bury-Bolton
    Bury - Rawtenstall
    Oldham-Rochdale

To assess the future potential of these five and the other 20 services the SELNEC Transportation Study, which had been set up by the local authorities in 1966 before the creation of SELNEC PTE, evaluated the closure proposals against a variety of land-use and other factors. Between the establishment of the PTE in 1969 and the conclusion of the Study in 1971 it was used by the PTE to evaluate and influence numerous public transport proposals. Suffice to say that none of them passed muster and the first four services were closed in 1970. The deficit on the Victoria-Oldham - Rochdale line was £438,000 p.a. It carried 2,300 weekday round trips generating £59,000 annually, but working costs were £497,000 - all at 1969 prices. The deficit per passenger mile was 3s 1d (15.13p), the second highest in the conurbation. Evaluation in the SELNEC Transportation Study Model showed it to have little value in the future. Nevertheless, there was great reluctance to close the Oldham-Rochdale line because of its perceived economic and social potential and from a political perspective. So the line has struggled on and is now - 40 years later - being incorporated into the Metrolink network.

The SELNEC Transportation Study evaluated numerous land use alternatives against a variety of highway and public transport plans, with a time horizon of 1984. A rapid transit line from Ringway (now Manchester) Airport to Langley near Middleton was evaluated as were a variety of railway upgradings and cross-Manchester tunnels. Eventually, the Picc-Vic Scheme emerged as the preferred public transport alternative. This would have involved bringing full-size railway trains from the Alderley Edge and Styal line services under the City Centre to Victoria and thence on to Bury and Bolton. Trains from Hazel Grove and Macclesfield would have run through the tunnel and terminated at Victoria. Subsequently, it was intended that they should be extended to Rochdale both via Oldham and Castleton. Parliamentary Powers were granted but the scheme fell foul of the economic crisis in 1973. Whilst scaled-back versions of the scheme were developed, together with rephasing, the PTA decided to drop the scheme in 1977.

Following abandonment of the Picc-Vic network, a Medium Term Rail Study identified a number of possible lower cost schemes to improve the local rail network. They included electrification of the Oldham-Rochdale line (not for the first time) at 25kV AC at a cost in the range £10m to £17m and the Castlefield Curve, now known as the Ordsall Curve, at a cost between £7m and £10m. A number of other electrification schemes were listed but the only one to be completed was from Stockport to Hazel Grove, in 1981. No other schemes from the study progressed beyond the planning stage.

British Railways had operated the lines in North Manchester on a shoestring, with no investment, minimum maintenance and a reduction in facilities, and this was particularly true of the Oldham-Rochdale route. The line had a dreadfully run-down appearance and was in a disgraceful state, as was recorded in the previous chapter. In 1982 the PTA, Greater Manchester Council (GMC) and BR accepted that this situation could not continue and, with government blessing, commenced The Greater Manchester Rail Strategy Study into the future of railways in the conurbation. The following year the first mention was made of converting the Oldham–Rochdale line to light rail. The evaluation included revisiting the Picc-Vic scheme and other alternative tunnel alignments, and also looked at the alternative of a surface link across the city centre, linking railway lines from the north with those in the south. This proposal to convert the Bury and Altrincham lines to light rail operation with street-running across the city centre, came out as the most cost-effective scheme, better than light rail in tunnels or conversion to busways. This became the Manchester Metrolink and Powers were obtained in 1988 (see Appendix 'A' for a full list or Metrolink's Parliamentary Powers). Details of the scheme and its development were set out in the Metrolink book, published in 1992, to celebrate the opening of Phase I by HM The Queen, on 17th July that year.

It had always been the intention that the Bury - Altrincham section would be the first of several lines to be connected across the city centre. The 1983 Feasibility Study proposed conversion to light rail of the existing rail lines to Bury, Altrincham, Glossop/Hadfield, Marple/Rose Hill, Rochdale via Oldham and the former Midland main line to East Didsbury. Altrincham and

Bury were selected as the first phase, together with the city centre links between Piccadilly, Victoria and G-Mex (the former Central Station) as the government would not accept building the six line network in one project. These lines produced the best rate of return because patronage was already high and the need for rolling stock and power supply renewal on the Bury line was urgent.

As implementation of the Phase I lines progressed, the routes to Glossop/Hadfield, Marple/Rose Hill and Oldham/Rochdale were overtaken by the new route to Salford Quays and Eccles, because of the need to attract private sector funding. New routes were also planned to Droylsden and Ashton and to Manchester Airport via Wythenshawe Town Centre and via Wythenshawe Hospital. Planning work on the Oldham/Rochdale line continued towards obtaining the necessary Parliamentary Powers. The dilatoriness of government policy, the abolition of Greater Manchester Council, and bus deregulation, both in 1986, delayed approval being given to follow up Metrolink's initial success with extensions and further conversions. The first extension, Phase 2, was to Salford Quays/Eccles for which Powers had been achieved in 1990. Nevertheless, a Bill to include Powers to convert the Victoria-Oldham-Rochdale line to Metrolink, was deposited in 1988 and was granted in the 1990 No 2 Act.

One of the reasons for the success of Metrolink is that it penetrates the heart of Manchester, giving direct access to work, shopping, social and educational opportunities, without the need to walk or take a bus or taxi from terminal railway stations like Victoria, Piccadilly or Oxford Road. Whilst it was known that this, together with greatly enhanced frequencies, would transform the value of the Oldham/Rochdale line, it was felt that this could be enhanced further if Metrolink ran through the centre of Oldham and was extended from Rochdale railway station (always remote from the town centre) to the town centre and bus station. Powers were sought for these two street running extensions in Bills promoted in 1989 and 1990. Powers were given for Rochdale in the 1991 Act and for Oldham in the 1993 Act.

Once again, the dilatoriness of successive government's transport policies ensured that no swift progress was made in moving these extensions forward. There was much discussion as to how the extensions should be funded and this, in turn, affected what type of contractual arrangement would be used to achieve the extensions. Phase 1 had been achieved through a DBOM (design, build, operate and maintain) type of contract, at the insistence of the then government. Amongst other things, this meant that the whole process would have to be gone through again for each extension, since it was not just a design and build contract, but also included operation and maintenance of the system subsequently built. The logical arrangement would have been to achieve extensions in phases under a design and build

arrangement, with the existing operator taking over the operation and, possibly, the maintenance, similar to the arrangements successfully used by Docklands Light Railway to achieve its extensions. Eventually, it was decided to achieve all the extensions in two phases, known as 3a and 3b. Phase 3a included Trafford Bar to St Werburgh's Road (Chorlton), Piccadilly to Droylsden and Victoria to Oldham and Rochdale, on the existing rail alignment.

Under the Transport Act 2000 local authorities and PTA/PTEs would be able to raise funds for public transport improvements by way of a Road User Charging Scheme (as then recently adopted in Central London) or by charging for private parking spaces. The Greater Manchester Authorities (bravely) developed a Road User Charging Scheme, which was put to a referendum in 2008. This was lost by a hefty majority of the public being against it which posed a major problem for the funding of the Metrolink extensions. Fortunately, the government - after intense local lobbying by local councillors - agreed that funds could be made available through the Greater Manchester Transport Fund, agreed with the Association of Greater Manchester Authorities (AGMA) and that loans could be raised on the back of future passenger revenues. Thus came about 'the big bang' whereby Phase 3a and 3b are combined for implementation, and the contract with M-Pact Thales extended accordingly.

It should be remembered that throughout this period the Oldham-Rochdale line had struggled on first with ancient DMUs and then with Pacers and Sprinters, with minimal maintenance to the infrastructure. Such is how we do things in Britain! By the time trams reach Rochdale town centre it will have taken nearly 30 years from the initial feasibility study, the same period of time that Rochdale Corporation's first generation electric trams operated!

A passer-by looks on as a Manchester-bound train crosses Beal Lane, Shaw in July 1980. The new crossing barriers are in place but not yet operational. *(RSG)*

CONVERSION TO METROLINK

Metrolink Phase I, the Bury-City-Altrincham route, had always been considered by the PTE as being the first step towards a much larger system, as was discussed in a previous chapter. The PTE had hoped that there would be a continuous programme of extensions, as would be the practice in Continental Europe or North America. Such continuity brings increasing benefits to people with additional areas being incorporated into the extensions, and, it also gives a continuous flow of work to experienced teams (subject to appropriate contractual arrangements). This in turn helps to contain costs. This did not happen in Manchester with the resultant gap of eight years between opening Phase I and the opening of the Eccles extension. There was a further gap of nine years from then to government approval for Phase 3a, which itself was subsequently amended to incorporate Phase 3b and the 'Big Bang'.

During these extended periods of constructional inactivity, technology moves on continuously and previous phases show signs of wear-and-tear, particularly as their costs were pared down to start with. Thus, further extensions were not simply add-ons to the existing system, but required modifications to it and the interfaces. Most obviously, new rolling stock is technologically more advanced so upgrades to existing systems are required. There is nothing worse for reliable operation than to have to interfere with it when building, testing and commissioning new trams or extensions. As will be discussed later, all these matters have a 'human element' in that staff have to be retrained and tested on operating or maintaining the new routes and equipment. Training takes time and resources away from the day-to-day job of operating the services.

So, in addition to building the Victoria-Oldham-Rochdale extensions following on from the Media City UK branch and the South Manchester line to St Werburgh's Road, Metrolink took delivery of new trams and commissioned them. It built a new depot at Trafford and recruited and trained staff to work there. It is also introducing a new Tram Management System which will, in due course, replace the automatic signalling on Phase I. These last two items will be dealt with later in this section.

Thus, the simple phrase 'conversion to Metrolink' covers a vast amount of work and processes. The state of the work depends largely on the condition of the existing assets. However, even well-maintained assets have to be brought up to current modern-day standards and to be fully compliant relating to all legislation covering the operation of a light railway. In particular the whole system needs to be fully compliant with the requirements of the Disability Discrimination Act (DDA) so that it is fully accessible to all people.

It should be remembered that the DDA requirements also offer great benefits to those who have pushchairs, buggies and prams, or are laden with shopping, as well as those with disabilities.

The Victoria-Oldham-Rochdale rail line had been run on a shoe-string for many years and most of the assets were in a very run-down state. Not only was it necessary to catch up on this backlog, to extend the life of structures by 50 years and to comply with all current legislation, it was also necessary to ensure that they would support reliable and trouble-free operation for the next 20 or so years. A strong case was put forward for a staged conversion, retaining a conventional rail service on the Shaw-Rochdale section, whilst work on the Manchester-Shaw section advanced but this was dismissed in favour of the convenience of being able to hand over the whole project to the contractors in one go.

Accordingly, the PTE decided to close the whole line for the conversion and this they did on 3rd October 2009, making the whole of the railway a working site, which is a lot easier from a contractor's point-of-view. However, it puts at risk future passenger estimates and, of course, is extremely inconvenient to current rail users. The PTE strenuously refused repeated requests for replacement bus services, claiming that the existing services provided an adequate alternative. Experience with the Bury and Altrincham line conversions in Phase 1 clearly made the PTE very cautious as those closure periods over-ran their timescales considerably. Nevertheless, 2½ years for the closure of the Victoria–Oldham-Rochdale line does seems somewhat excessive, given that the conversion of the Bury line took less than eight months, even with over-run and Altrincham less than six months.

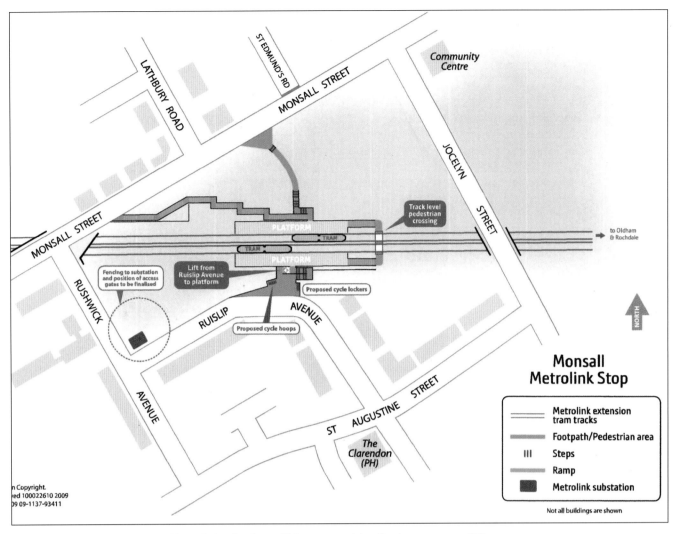

The layout of the new tram stop at Monsall showing the multiple access points with steps, ramps and lifts.

Map labels:

LATHBURY ROAD

ST EDMUND'S RD

MONSALL STREET

Community Centre

JOCELYN STREET

MONSALL STREET

PLATFORM

TRAM

TRAM

PLATFORM

Track level pedestrian crossing

to Oldham & Rochdale

Fencing to substation and position of access gates to be finalised

Lift from Ruislip Avenue to platform

Proposed cycle lockers

RUSHWICK

RUISLIP AVENUE

Proposed cycle hoops

AVENUE

ST AUGUSTINE STREET

The Clarendon (PH)

NORTH

Monsall Metrolink Stop

———	Metrolink extension tram tracks
▒	Footpath/Pedestrian area
III	Steps
▒	Ramp
■	Metrolink substation

Not all buildings are shown

Access to platforms from surrounding streets is crucial to the attractiveness of the Metrolink system. Over the years British Rail had reduced access to many stations by restricting it to one point. With Metrolink's self-service approach to ticketing it is possible to have multiple access points to better serve the surrounding area. However, each access must offer level or ramped approaches to platforms, where necessary, with a more direct stepped approach for able-bodied passengers. Where ramps would be of excessive length, lifts have to be provided. Not only is this expensive but it also provides a target for vandals and assaults. All approaches have to be lit and many are covered by CCTV surveillance.

Once the track-bed had been made good, clean ballast was put down followed by the new track on concrete blocks with steel tie-rods. Cross-overs between tracks and other point-and-crossing work need to be laid and the whole lot welded up into long-lengths with expansion switches, at appropriate locations. The track is tamped and fine-lined throughout the route, with very tight tolerances being demanded through platforms, bridges and tunnels.

The state of the track on the existing railway was such that it was decided to lay new track throughout the route. However, before this could be done it was important to give attention to track drainage and the track-bed and ensurie such ballast as remained was clean. Attention to embankments and cuttings for any sign of movement and erosion was necessary and over a hundred structures on the line required attention to some degree. Apart from bridges over or under motorways or recently constructed roads, they were almost all more then 100 years old and all iron or steel bridges had suffered from some degree of corrosion.

The condition of the bridges was found to be considerably worse than had been expected. This led to the need for additional strengthening works on some arched overbridges and deck replacement on some underbridges. This increased the costs of the works and led to the lengthening of the construction programme. Fortunately, the two tunnels at Oldham appeared sound.

There were only two major bridge works. Firstly, the new flyover bridge taking the Metrolink alignment across the heavy rail tracks at Thorpes Bridge. This spectacular pre-stressed structure is integral with Central Park stop. It makes a public statement about the Metrolink's presence. The other major bridge is a new steel structure but at a big skew over the heavy rail line at Rochdale East Junction.

The spectacular multi-curved flyover which carries the Metrolink line over the Calder Valley line south of Thorpes Bridge. The pylon of Central Park tram stop can be seen in the background. *(DSH)*

Ground level view of the futuristic tram stop at Central Park, *(DSH)*

Whilst most stations on the existing line are being retained they require substantial work to bring them up to Metrolink requirements. All platforms must be 915 mm. above rail level to ensure level boarding/ alighting between a Metrolink car and the platform; also throughout the length of the vehicle (and double-unit operation must be provided for) 60m of platform face must present a gap between platform face and car floor of 40 mm This is a very exacting standard to construct and maintain, but crucial for the safe usage of wheelchairs, buggies, etc. Platforms require re-surfacing, fencing and lighting with the provision of waiting shelters, ticket vending machines (TVMs), CCTV, etc, as considered appropriate.

Once the track had been completed it was then possible to erect the overhead line equipment (OHLE) bases and poles before the final stringing of the wire. Sub-stations for distribution of power over the system and feeders from the national grid had also to be constructed at suitable locations. Fortunately, the use of 750v dc overhead power, and the smaller profile of light rail vehicles, permitted electrification of existing railway lines without substantial rebuilding of bridges or track lowering.

The route

The new Metrolink route follows the Bury line through Collyhurst tunnel to Irk Valley Junction where it diverges to take the spur to join the Manchester Loop at Smedley Viaduct Junction, where there is a connection back to Queens Road depot to enable trams to run on or off service from the Rochdale direction. It then follows the former loop line on a rising gradient along a deep cutting and through Rochdale Road tunnel to the first stop at Monsall, lying between Monsall Street and Jocelyn Street.

After Monsall the next new stop is at Central Park to serve this rapidly expanding development area which includes new headquarters for Greater Manchester Police. Central Park, too, has two side platforms, and is of spectacular design with a circular overall roof. It is accessed from The Gateway, the main approach from Oldham Road. A lay-by for buses is provided off The Gateway. There is lift access to each platform. This station was built in 2005 at the cost of £35m, including the bridge, although it was not used until

2012. Such was the delay to authorising the project. There then follows the spectacular inverted 'T' pre-stressed concrete bridge which incorporates vertical and horizontal curves to take double track Metrolink over Thorpes Bridge Junction and on to the Oldham line proper. Shortly after the Metrolink line becomes single, taking over the erstwhile Up line for the next mile (see cover). This is to permit the retention of the line to access the Greater Manchester Authority's Refuse and Waste Disposal Facilities, which are served by the regular 'Bin Line' trains. The Metrolink line returns to double track beyond this point.

On this single line section is found the stop for 'Newton Heath and Moston' on the site of the former Dean Lane two-platform railway station. A much extended ramp provides disabled access to the Metrolink platform. Now back on the Oldham line proper, the next stop is Failsworth, where the former station has been rebuilt with lift access provided to each platform from Hardman Lane. The line continues to the refurbished bridge over the Rochdale Canal, and onto the Hollinwood stop. Once again, the former railway station has been rebuilt to Metrolink standards. It is accessed from Hollinwood Avenue by a road loop off Stable Street and Railway Road. Because the line is on an embankment at this location, lifts are provided to each platform from the road loop or Hudson Street, which has been closed to motor vehicles. A major park-and-ride facility has been built including a multi-storey car park.

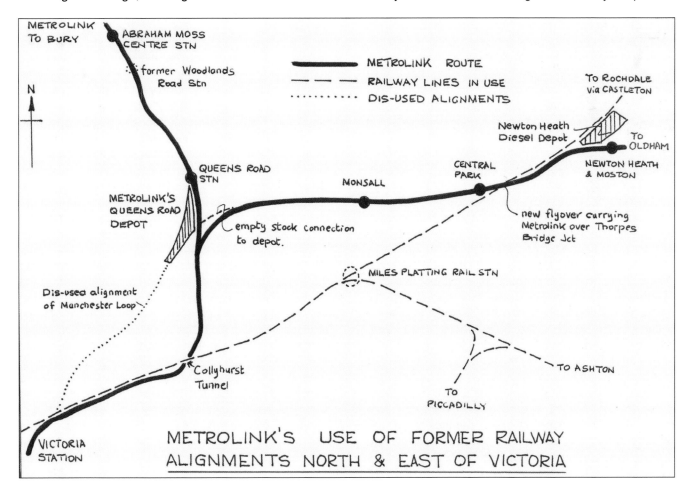

METROLINK'S USE OF FORMER RAILWAY ALIGNMENTS NORTH & EAST OF VICTORIA

From the temporary Mumps terminus the route will cross the former roundabout and run up Brook Street to rejoin the old alignment. The new town centre line will come in from the left. *(DSH)*

Immediately north of Hollinwood station is the large bridge carrying Metrolink over both Hollinwood Avenue and the M60. Being of recent construction, this required little attention. The next stop at South Chadderton is a new one located adjacent to Coalshaw Green Park, accessed by footpaths from Coalshaw Green Road and Canal Street with potential additional links into the proposed Rose Hill development site and adjacent area. The original alignment was on an embankment. This has been removed and the track realigned so it is at ground level with an at-grade level crossing.

Another new stop named Freehold has been built where the existing alignment crosses Block Lane. A new footbridge has been built over Block Lane, connecting the two platforms via a pedestrian crossing and there are separate lifts to each platform.

The new street-running alignment through Oldham Town Centre leaves the existing line immediately after the Featherstall Road Bridge, where it swings off northwards, as the original line goes straight into Werneth station. The Town Centre section will be dealt with later. Werneth station was demolished since the railway alignment was considered to have no future after the opening of the new route through the town centre. This is a contentious issue, since retention of the existing direct line would offer faster journeys for those coming from north of Oldham, and provide a diversionary route to the Town Centre route when required.

For the time being, in order to bring the benefits of Metrolink to Oldham and Rochdale as soon as possible, the remainder of the former alignment has been converted to Metrolink operation with no intermediate stops. The conversion involves reconditioning the existing track and putting up the overhead wiring through Werneth and Central tunnels. Oldham Mumps station has been demolished and replaced by a new temporary island platform and reversing crossover just west of the site of the old station.

The former railway, which used to cross Mumps Bridge and the roundabout on a pair of bridges, has been demolished and a totally new traffic-signalled junction installed. The new town centre route rejoins the former railway alignment immediately adjacent to Brook Street.

Oldham Town Centre

The new alignment leaves the former railway line immediately after passing under Featherstall Road South. It curves sharply northward to the level of, and parallel to, Featherstall Road South. As it approaches Middleton Road it turns again, sharply, eastward to run parallel to that road. At this point there is the stop 'Westwood' which has two side platforms. From here the line runs parallel until Middleton Road's junction with the Ring Road (Oldham Way). The tracks then curve right and run parallel to the exit slip road from the elevated section of Oldham Way, before crossing the roundabout at ground level under the Ring Road.

Metrolink then follows a tricky alignment curving, climbing and passing under John Street to the King Street stop, which is off-street, immediately before the junction of King Street and Union Street West. This stop has two side platforms at ground level. The alignment continues along Union Street. The next stop – the 'new' Oldham Central – is an island platform in the middle of a pedestrianised section of Union Street. Metrolink continues along Union Street to its junction with Yorkshire Street and so to the new Mumps stop. This is a major interchange with bus stands either side of a two platform layout, all of which is off-street. There is also a park-and-ride car park for about 250 cars. The alignment then swings away to the north to pick up the former railway alignment climbing up to it, parallel to Brook Street.

Oldham Mumps to Rochdale Station (under construction)

Once again the former rail alignment is converted to Metrolink, with all the stations being rebuilt as Metrolink stops. The single line section north of Shaw and Crompton is being re-doubled. The first stop is Derker with a two-sided platform layout where a lift is being installed between Yates Street and the outbound platform. Substantial redevelopment is anticipated adjacent to this stop and provision is being made for park-and-ride.

The line continues to the next stop at Shaw & Crompton where substantial changes have been made. The former railway station lay to the north of Beal Lane, whereas the new Metrolink stop lies south of it. It will have three platform faces, the inbound platform being an island with a Manchester-facing bay platform. The former footbridge has been removed and the level crossing reduced to a typical traffic light-controlled road crossing. Substantial park-and-ride provision is made adjacent to the site of the old station.

At Newhey the station has been rebuilt to Metrolink standards with the former down (now outbound) platform brought back into use. The re-doubled line then continues under the M62 to Milnrow, which has been upgraded to Metrolink standards as with Newhey. The station is immediately adjacent to Elizabethan Way, the link road from the M62 to Rochdale, for those coming from the east. The line continues towards Rochdale with a new stop to serve the new Kingsway Business Park. It then crosses the Rochdale Canal and Kingsway to another new stop at Newbold to serve recent development in the area, including a superstore. Newbold has an island platform. After leaving this stop the line singles to cross over Milnrow Road on the existing single track railway bridge and then by a large, new, skew bridge, crosses Rochdale East Junction. The alignment descends to existing track level and reaches ground level in front of Rochdale Station using the former High Level Road. Station Road is substantially re-aligned. Metrolink becomes double track again, before curving sharp right (north) to reach Rochdale Station stop on Maclure Road. This stop has an island platform.

Construction of the Metrolink line approaching Rochdale Station has involved the demolition of the Rochdale East Junction signal box and wholesale, overdue, re-signalling of the Calder Valley heavy rail line. This is now controlled by a new box (Rochdale West) at Castleton, opened in 2011.

Rochdale Town Centre

The alignment continues along Maclure Road and then runs alongside Drake Street to Wet Rake Gardens and then with street running all the way down Drake Street to the town centre. Drake Street between Water Street and Smith Street will be tram and pedestrian only except for southbound buses. There will be a short section of single track between Drake Street and the terminus. The island platform terminal, approached by a scissor crossover, is immediately adjacent to the existing Bus Station and Council Offices. There are 18 stops in the 15¾ miles (25.3km) from Victoria to Rochdale Town Centre. These are listed in Appendix 'B'. Nine are new for Metrolink, showing the improved accessibility provided by light rail. The proposal to have a stop on Drake Street was abandoned on cost grounds. A new transport interchange is being built on the south side of Smith Street, and the existing bus station, multi-storey car park and 'Black Box' council offices will be demolished.

Location and Control of Trams

The signalling, control and supervision of trams on the section from Irk Valley Junction through Oldham to Rochdale Town Centre has always posed a challenge to Metrolink planners and designers. Had the former railway alignment been adhered to throughout to Rochdale Station, it is likely that it would have been re-signalled with the simple automatic system adopted for the Bury and Altrincham lines. Line-of-sight (LOS) operation would have been used on the street-running section to Rochdale Town Centre. This assumes light rail as opposed to tramway operation.

As soon as it was decided to serve Oldham Town Centre, where street-running would apply, the situation became more complex. Clearly LOS was appropriate for this section but drivers would have then been faced with switching four times between entering the signalled section at Victoria and arriving at Rochdale Town Centre. This would be very confusing, particularly in dark or foggy weather, where a driver could feel temporarily 'lost'.

It made sense, therefore, to adopt LOS driving for the whole branch from Irk Valley Junction. Furthermore, apart from the two Oldham tunnels, forward vision was good and there were no 'railway' junctions, so speed and running times should not be affected. LOS was to be adopted for the whole length of the East line to Droylsden and Ashton and would be adopted once clear of the Depot access points at Trafford Bar on the East Didsbury/Airport lines.

In the original planning of Metrolink Phase 1, it was decided to adopt a simple form of automatic signalling for the segregated sections, i.e. from Bury to Victoria and from Deansgate/Castlefield (formerly GMex) to Altrincham. This was to be in a two-aspect system with automatic tram-stops to apply brakes when necessary at each signal. At certain locations, because of sighting problems, repeater signals had to be installed. The signalling on the segregated sections was designed for 3-minute headways and, at the inner ends, from Queens Road to Victoria, and from GMex to Trafford Bar, for 1½ minute headways. At the time (1988) these headways were thought to be sufficient to cope with the anticipated expansion of the system.

However, it is now clear that shorter headways will be required for the system's ultimate development. This could only be achieved by re-signalling and a considerable degree of sophistication, which was not necessary for the majority of the system, as it was now to be operated on Line-of-Sight (LOS) principles.

Furthermore, having regard to the fact that all the signalling equipment on the Bury and Altrincham line was now at least 20 years old, with increasing maintenance costs and decreasing reliability, and that most of the future Metrolink network would be operated on LOS principles, it made sense to scrap the existing signalling in favour of a new Tram Management System (TMS) to supervise operations. This, of course, increased substantially the scope and the cost of Phase 3, but it also introduced additional interfaces with the two tram fleets and Phase 1 infrastructure interface issues have been discussed before and provide a major challenge to all involved, particularly when they are safety-critical. It is fair to say that Metrolink, and its contractors, have struggled to cope and this has led to some delays to opening dates.

The TMS requires a bespoke configuration at each interface between the existing system and the new TMS. The first section to be so controlled was from Pomona, via Media City UK, to Eccles. This solution cannot be simply applied elsewhere on the network. The new TMS represents a significant change in the supervision and control of the expanded Metrolink network, as will be described later. Driver and Control Room staff need to be trained and become familiar and confident with the new operating methods to ensure safe operation of each section. The order of conversion established was: Trafford Depot and access/egress thereto; Cornbrook, Victoria and Irk Valley Junction.

With specific regard to the Oldham-Rochdale line there are complex interface issues with Phase 1 at Queens Road and Irk Valley junctions, and with Network Rail regarding access to the Waste Disposal Site at Dean Lane.

New Tram Management System

The new Tram Management System (TMS) is based upon two operational principles. Firstly, that trams are driven on Line-of-Sight (LOS) operation and secondly, that trams pass through or across junctions on a first-come-first-served basis. The first means that the maximum speed at which a tram can be safely driven is governed by the driver's view ahead or to the side of him, when approaching trailing junctions. Where the angle of approach is shallow the driver is given additional assistance as described later. The driver cannot assume the line ahead is clear, as can be done with block or automatic signalling. At all times the driver must be able to stop within his LOS, should there be another tram or vehicle blocking his path. If the Controller wishes to alter the sequence of trams, or re-form the service, he can lock the signals approaching a junction. Alternatively, he could intervene by radio contact to instruct a driver to wait at a specific position clear of a junction. It is critical that the passenger information system on each platform is capable of handling all the information relating to the sequence and destinations of approaching trams.

If there is no possibility of a conflicting movement, e.g. Trafford Bar Outbound, there will be a points indicator and no signal. Where there is a signal its normal aspect would be 'stop', i.e. a horizontal white bar. It would only clear to a 'proceed' aspect (vertical white bar) if the anticipated route is clear across the junction. In other words, the TMS has checked that there is no approaching tram on the other line or other conflicting movement. The route for the approaching tram will then be set and locked and the approach signal cleared. The points indicator will confirm the lie of the points. In the Metrolink system there will be several junction-specific solutions. Where the speed on the route to be followed by the approaching tram is significantly lower than the route from which the tram is turning off, the signal controlling the junction will show a *diagonal white line* warning the driver to reduce speed.

Each tram has an on-board computer, which carries all the route and topographical data for the Metrolink network. The tram's computer also contains that particular tram's runnings for the day. This is uploaded via the radio in the depot before the tram runs out on to its first duty of the day.

A tram computes its location from the last physical loop passed, updated by the odometer. On passing a trackside radio beacon this is transmitted to the Central Control, hence the position of each tram is known. The whole of the network is covered by a mesh radio system, the purpose of which is the passage of data between trams and Central Control and vice-versa.

According to Thales, the supplier of the system, this is one of the first examples of mesh radio being used on a tram system. It allows the Controller to get more frequent updates, so necessary for the accurate prediction of a tram's location on a system of complex junctions and frequent services. The new Central Control Room, which also forms part of Thales' contract, will be located at the new depot and will, in due course, replace the original Control Room at Queens Road. The Central Control will also feature a network-wide SCADA system and CCTV monitoring. The SCADA (Systems Control and Diagnostic Advice) system allows power supplies, lifts, wayside apparatus, etc. to be monitored and controlled centrally. The CCTV ensures passenger safety throughout Metrolink, by monitoring tram stops, ticket machines, car parks, etc.

All points have an induction loop on their approach. This loop ensures the correct lie of the points, that they are locked for the approaching tram and remain locked during the passage of the whole train (or consist) in the case of two-car operation.

Most of the physical loops are Stop Line detector loops, since this is a known position and a tram can proceed up to this point in LOS operation, with no fear of conflict. Other loops on the approach side of a junction are virtual loops created within the on-board computer and representing, for example: Advance, Prepare or Clearance loops in a real system. The creation of these virtual loops within the vehicle's computer is done having regard to the distance passed since the last real loop. Through the mesh radio system the tram transmits its location. Thus the Central Control, through the TMS, ensures that the correct route is selected and locked, and the points indicator shows the driver the route set, effectively replicating a conventional tram management system, but in electronic or e-format. TMS also controls tram priority at numerous city centre junctions and routes the tram through all junctions. also drives the passenger information system.

It is claimed that the new TMS improves operating performance and reduces the amount of hardware to be installed on or around the track, reducing costs, and susceptibility to vandalism. Whether the claimed savings are achieved in all weathers, and at acceptable levels of reliability, remains to be seen. There is no doubt that it is complex and a great deal has to be computed quickly on a moving tram, as it approaches a junction. This is, of course, particularly crucial where trams are approaching from the other direction and a conflicting movement has to be avoided. In 'desk-top conditions' this might be achievable but will it work with trams having a closing speed of say, 60 mph, let alone the line-speed maximum of 50 x 2, i.e. 100 mph? Introducing speed limits for trams approaching junctions is unsatisfactory from a journey-time viewpoint. This is one of the differences between tramways and light railways, the former having to accept a compromise.

It is understood that at major junctions on the segregated sections, where speed limits are higher than on the street-running section, (for example: Irk Valley Junction, Cornbrook and Trafford Bar), the Outer or Advance loop will usually be a real physical loop. It is this loop that triggers the whole sequence for the approaching tram to pass safely over or through the junction ahead. For the safe and efficient operation of the Metrolink system it is essential that these Outer or Advanced loops, where they exist, are positioned so that the approaching tram can run through the junction at the line speed for the route set. This may be a tall order. The stop-line detector will always be a real loop.

When approaching junctions at a shallow angle there will be a 'signal passed at stop' (SPAS) system. If a potential 'hit' is detected a line of blue lights will immediately start to flash and the drivers of approaching trams must stop immediately. A similar arrangement is proposed for single-line sections (which is a system used in Croydon Tramlink). Whilst it may be applicable in Croydon's circumstances, one wonders if it is suitable at such locations as Irk Valley Junction, Cornbrook

or Trafford Bar, where line speeds (with conventional signalling) are much higher. In future speeds will have to be lower.

Traditionally, trams are driven on line-of-sight (LOS) principles. The situation is much less clear-cut with light railways, where tracks are largely segregated and speeds are higher. In developing light rail systems it is important to achieve the simplicity of LOS operation, but if this can only be achieved by imposing additional and/or lower speed limits than could be achieved with a simple signalling system, the object would be self-defeating. Also, such operation can put added pressure on the driver.

Considerable lengths of the Bury line and certain sections of the Altrincham line have reduced sight lines due to vertical and/or horizontal curvature of the alignment, location of bridge structures and vegetation (although the latter can be controlled). Extensive tests have been carried out to determine the maximum speed a tram could proceed within LOS and still be able to stop clear of a tram in front. Details are not yet available as to the lower speed limits that would have to be introduced, and hence the effect on journey time (and the number of trams) cannot yet be calculated. To have endless, varying speed limit signs seems a recipe for confusion for the driver.

An alternative being considered is to have variable speed limit signs at certain locations and in some tunnels, thus allowing trams to follow each other with a closer spacing than would otherwise be possible. There will also be an in-cab display to assist the driver in keeping to time. Normally, it would display the speed limit for LOS driving. However, if a second tram is following rather close to a preceding tram, the system would calculate a lower maximum speed and display it. Such signs would have flashing lights, similar to those on motorways. It will be crucial for the driver to react immediately to such signs.

All systems relying on LOS principles are influenced by the weather, particularly fog, sleet and snow. It relies on the driver to adjust his/her speed accordingly, and there is a considerable variation in driver perception, as any motorist knows. Sections of the Bury line, between Radcliffe and Bury, and the Altrincham line in the Mersey Valley, are particularly susceptible to mist and fog. It will be interesting to see how the Tram Management System copes. In a report to the TfGM Committee dated 1st March 2012, the Metrolink Director, Phil Purdey, wrote, "In developing the bespoke requirements at the major rail junctions on the network, a number of technical complexities have emerged that have delayed the rollout of the TMS across the network. The technical interfaces between equipment required to identify vehicle location, onboard vehicle equipment, the control of the infrastructure and signals is complex and needs to be robust to ensure a safe operational system. These complexities have required detailed rework and testing to meet requirements which have resulted in delays in migrating the system across the network.

The tram fleet

At Phase 1 there were 26 T68 trams, but with the opening of the Eccles branch a further 6 T68A trams were added. The original fleet was not allowed to operate on the Eccles line, which was defined as a tramway, without a number of modifications, including altered braking arrangements and a collapsible and shrouded coupling at each end. Since street-running was practised in Manchester City Centre with all the T68s this restriction for the Eccles line seemed unreasonable but the ban had to be accepted which meant there were no spare vehicles for the Eccles line.

Initially the T68As were less reliable than their predecessors at the same stage of development, and reliability on the 12-minute frequency service was often unacceptable. In the end eight T68s were modified for operation on the Eccles line so, in effect, the 32-strong fleet is made up of three components: T68s, modified T68s and T68As, making reliable operation of an intensively used fleet (peak vehicle demand 29) very difficult and expensive to achieve. The introduction of yet another type of vehicle, the new Bombardier-built M5000, would have added to problems and, whilst they could have been concentrated upon the new lines, there would still be inter-working over common sections, notably in the City Centre.

The complexities of the mixed fleet were anticipated by the operator in the 1998-2005 period, and a number of desk-studies were undertaken to retire early the older vehicles, then only six years old. A financial case could never be made, but fifteen years on the T68s are over 20 years old and the T68A 10 years old, with reliability problems of significant proportions. Furthermore, Bombardier have a production line, in Vienna, of M5000s, rolling out a tram-per-month and the fact that the design is one of a family with components common to vehicles in Croydon and Cologne, helps. In November 2011 it was decided to scrap the T68/T68A fleet and order a further 12 M5000s for delivery in 2013/14. The old vehicles will be progressively replaced and all have been refurbished to some degree and reliability varies within the fleet. It is anticipated that a further 20 new trams will be required in due course, especially if traffic forecasts are achieved.

The new trams

Bombardier is supplying the fleet of new trams for the Metrolink extensions. These are designated M5000 and are part of their range which already operate extensively on the Continent. They are built at Bombardier's plant in Vienna, Austria. They are very similar to the K5000, high-floor trams built for Cologne. Electrically both they and Cologne's low-floor K4000 are similar, with the electrical equipment supplied by Kiepe of Dusseldorf. (The K4000 is the same design as supplied to Croydon Tramlink.) It is interesting to note that the original Metrolink system had been designed around the Duwag-built German Stadtbahn B-car that

was the standard light rail vehicle for the Land of North-Rhein Westfalia. This design also influenced greatly the Tyne and Wear Metro cars. Unfortunately, the Consortium building Phase 1 of Metrolink did not offer these German built vehicles. The Stadtbahn B-cars are now being replaced by the new Bombardier design. So, 24 years later, Metrolink is getting the vehicle for which it was designed!

A general arrangement drawing of the new tram is shown opposite. The overall length of an M5000 is 28.4m, 2.65m wide and with an overall height of 3.67m. It is a two-section articulated vehicle carried on three bogies, the outer two each being powered by two 120 kW, air-cooled, 3-phase asynchronous motors. It takes power at 750v dc from the overhead. The vehicle has a maximum speed of 80 km/h (50 mph) with an acceleration rate when fully loaded of 1.08 m/s². It has four braking systems: a generatonic (regenerative) electrical service brake; a disc-operated manual service brake; a magnetic track brake (for emergencies) and a disc parking brake. The bogies have rubber/metal primary suspension with coil springs for secondary suspension. The bogies incorporate slip-slide protection, flange lubrication and sanders. The maximum axle load is 10.45 tonnes, and the vehicles can climb 65% (1 in 15.3) gradients and negotiate 25m radius curves.

The M5000s have a driver's cab at each end and a central, roof-mounted pantograph. There are four double sliding plug doors on each side of the vehicle, with a width of 1305mm. The empty vehicle's weight is 39.7 tonnes (10 tonnes lighter than a T68). There is an air cooling system for the passenger compartment and the driver's cabs are air-conditioned. The carrying capacity of each tram is 206 passengers of whom 60 are seated. There is standing capacity for 146 passengers. There are two spaces for prams/wheelchairs. Trams are normally run as single units, but are operated in pairs in peak periods and for special events. Up to four units can be coupled together in an emergency, but platforms are only capable of accommodating two units.

Seventy-four trams are currently on order. An initial batch of eight was ordered in April 2007, with an option of purchasing up to 97 vehicles. A second batch of four was ordered in October. An order was placed for the third batch of 28 June 2008. A fourth batch of eight was ordered in March 2010, followed by a fifth batch of 14 in August that year. When it was decided in November 2011 to replace the T68As (six vehicles) and some of the T68s, a further 12 trams were ordered.

Alterations at Queens Road

The original Metrolink maintenance depot at Queens Road was built with an eye to further expansion. So as part of the Phase 3a works it has been expanded, with the provision of additional sidings, a second washing machine and a sand dispensing plant. A second entry point has been provided from Smedley Viaduct, where

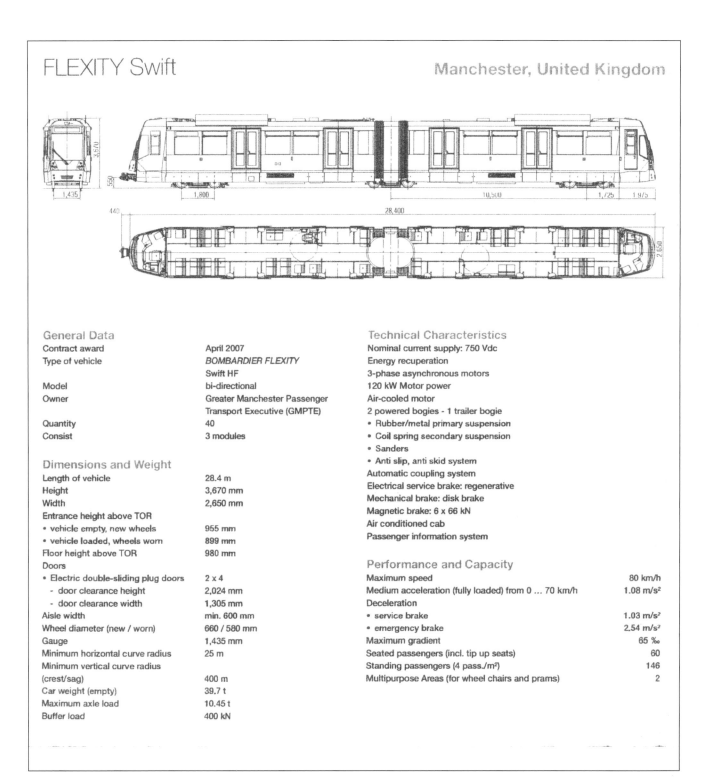

FLEXITY Swift

Manchester, United Kingdom

General Data

Contract award	April 2007
Type of vehicle	*BOMBARDIER FLEXITY*
	Swift HF
Model	bi-directional
Owner	Greater Manchester Passenger
	Transport Executive (GMPTE)
Quantity	40
Consist	3 modules

Dimensions and Weight

Length of vehicle	28.4 m
Height	3,670 mm
Width	2,650 mm
Entrance height above TOR	
• vehicle empty, new wheels	955 mm
• vehicle loaded, wheels worn	899 mm
Floor height above TOR	980 mm
Doors	
• Electric double-sliding plug doors	2 x 4
- door clearance height	2,024 mm
- door clearance width	1,305 mm
Aisle width	min. 600 mm
Wheel diameter (new / worn)	660 / 580 mm
Gauge	1,435 mm
Minimum horizontal curve radius	25 m
Minimum vertical curve radius	
(crest/sag)	400 m
Car weight (empty)	39.7 t
Maximum axle load	10.45 t
Buffer load	400 kN

Technical Characteristics

Nominal current supply: 750 Vdc
Energy recuperation
3-phase asynchronous motors
120 kW Motor power
Air-cooled motor
2 powered bogies - 1 trailer bogie
• Rubber/metal primary suspension
• Coil spring secondary suspension
• Sanders
• Anti slip, anti skid system
Automatic coupling system
Electrical service brake: regenerative
Mechanical brake: disk brake
Magnetic brake: 6 x 66 kN
Air conditioned cab
Passenger information system

Performance and Capacity

Maximum speed	80 km/h
Medium acceleration (fully loaded) from 0 ... 70 km/h	1.08 m/s²
Deceleration	
• service brake	1.03 m/s²
• emergency brake	2.54 m/s²
Maximum gradient	65 ‰
Seated passengers (incl. tip up seats)	60
Standing passengers (4 pass./m²)	146
Multipurpose Areas (for wheel chairs and prams)	2

the spur comes down from Irk Valley Junction, under the Bury line viaduct to near the site of Cheetham Hill Junction. This permits trams to run directly on or off the Oldham/Rochdale line, thus avoiding the need to travel to or from Victoria. Substantial alterations to the Control Room at Queens Road were also required to accommodate the new TMS system. Ultimately, the Control will be transferred to the new depot at Trafford. The staff halt at Queens Road will be rebuilt as a normal Metrolink stop for public use.

The new depot

When the Metrolink 'Big Bang' is completed the tram fleet will consist of around 100 vehicles and it was clear that a second depot would be required. The most obvious site was one that lay in the 'V' of the junction of the Altrincham and East Didsbury lines immediately south of Trafford Bar stop. This was a flat site but completely built upon with mills, factories and warehouses, many unused or unoccupied. It had good road access from Elsinore Road and Argyll Road and tramway access from both the Altrincham and Didsbury

The New Trafford Depot

New M5000 class tram 3046 is shown under inspection with the front skirt raised to expose the automatic coupling. *(DSH)*

The new depot is situated adjacent to the Old Trafford tram stop in the V between the Altrincham and South Manchester lines. The picture above, taken in September 2009, shows work progressing on putting in the services. Six months later, in March 2010, work has progressed and the main running shed is rising up from the mud. *(Both CR)*

Above, another of the same class, number 3030 is shown over the pits and under the inspection gantry, while below the latest delivery, trams number 3042 and the as yet un-numbered 3058 stand in the sidings together with earlier deliveries on the left and withdrawn T68s awaiting disposal on the right. *(Both DSH)*

This view inside the new depot taken In October 2012 shows the spacious layout with the new pits in the foreground and the gantry for roof inspection in the middle distance. *(DSH)*

More new trams

Above: A line-up of the new M5000 trams stored at the new Trafford depot.

Upper right: The cab layout. *(Bom)*

Lower right: Interior view of half a vehicle through the wide articulation, showing the 2+1 seating and generous circulating areas. *(Bom)*

Below: In basic yellow and not yet numbered, unit number 3003 stands in Queens Road depot soon after delivery. *(CR)*

lines and was convenient for the potential workforce. It also provided a depot on the south side of the City. The Secretary of State granted compulsory powers and planning permission for the new depot to the PTE in April 2002. The new depot has capacity for 96 trams and was opened in 2011.

Park and Ride

The 'Big Bang' allows the PTE to undertake a complete upgrading of Metrolink Phase 1 and 2, as well as constructing the Phase 3 works. There is little doubt that Phase 1 works were pared down to save costs before the then government would approve the scheme in 1988. This was particularly evident to the minimalist refurbishment of stations, the inadequate passenger information system and the lack of park and ride provision.

This latter point was particularly galling since passenger forecasts had assumed a significant amount of car parking at key stations such as Bury, Radcliffe, Whitefield, Prestwich, Sale and Altrincham. Apart from Radcliffe, Metrolink's provision of park and ride spaces was virtually non-existent. Much later the PTE found it possible to build a large car park at Whitefield.

The 'Big Bang' now allows this situation to be rectified and thus further integrate Metrolink into the transportation infrastructure of the area. New or enhanced sites are proposed for: Dane Road, Prestwich, Whitefield, Radcliffe, Ashton Moss, Ashton West, Derker, Hollinwood, Mumps, Rochdale Railway Station, Shaw and Crompton, East Didsbury and Sale Water Park. Some of these may be developed as multi-storey car parks. Well in excess of 2,000 parking places will be provided. This is a significant and long-overdue development.

Phased opening

Although the 'Big Bang' was approved late in 2010, it was always intended to open the new extensions in phases. The order of opening was:

> Harbour City to Media City UK
> Trafford Bar to St Werburgh's Road
> Irk Valley Junction to Central Park
> Piccadilly to Velodrome
> Central Park to Oldham Mumps
> Velodrome to Droylsden
> Mumps to Rochdale Station
> Droylsden to Ashton-under-Lyne
> St Werburgh's Road to East Didsbury
> Oldham Town Centre
> Rochdale Town Centre

There was also the building and the commissioning of the new depot at Trafford in time to accept the first

of the new M5000 trams which were delivered in 2009, alterations to Queens Road Depot and alterations to the Control Room at Queens Road.

Whilst the order of opening is being achieved, dates have slipped consistently. Delivery of the infrastructure is in general on time as are the new tram deliveries. The problems relate to the new TMS and, particularly, its interface with existing systems, as has been discussed previously. Physical hardware has to be in place and commissioned and the multitude of computer systems must also work in a safe and satisfactory manner before staff training can commence.

The original opening dates for Metrolink, including the Oldham - Rochdale line were:

To Central Park and Mumps (temporary stop)	
	Opened Spring 2012
Piccadilly to Droylsden	2012
Mumps - Rochdale Railway Station	Autumn 2012
Droylsden – Ashton	Winter 2013/14
Oldham & Rochdale Town Centres	2014

In the March 2012 report to TfGM, to which reference has already been made, suggested an opening to Rochdale Railway Station in summer 2012 is now likely to be subject to a three to six month delay, because of the TMS issues. Opening to Droylsden is also delayed by three months, to autumn 2012. even these extended dates were not achieved. The opening to Mumps was on 13th June 2012 and to Droylsden on 11th February 2013.

Once the route through Oldham Town Centre has been completed, it is proposed to abandon the former railway section from Werneth to the temporary terminus at Mumps. The track and OHLE will be recovered and re-used on the Airport branch. This also implies doing further road-works at Mumps and plain-lining the track there, although track slab has been provided for both direct and Town Centre services. However, it must be questioned as to the sense of scrapping the former direct link from Mumps to Freehold, having incurred substantial expenditure, probably at least £20m. It provides a diversionary route if or when the Town Centre line is blocked. It offers the potential of running a direct (and hence faster) service from Shaw and Crompton to Victoria. However, it is claimed that the five or six minutes saved would pose timetabling problems from Freehold inwards. Others claim that there are operating strategies that would overcome such problems. The two stops at Mumps could cause passenger some confusion. For reliable operation it is essential that trams present themselves from the Oldham line at six-minute intervals. In February 2012 work on the major utilities between Rochdale Station and the Town Centre terminus had been completed.

METROLINK OPERATION

One feature of Metrolink's operations is the simplicity of the service pattern, the ease of interchange between routes and that all trams stop at all stops. This latter feature is particularly important to irregular travellers who do not have to worry whether or not the tram will stop for them to board or alight, particularly in the dark.

The PTE's original specification for the service was to link Bury with Piccadilly and Altrincham with Piccadilly, throughout the day, every 10 minutes with a five-minute service being run in the peak periods on Mondays to Fridays. When planning the operation of the first section to open from Bury to Victoria it was found that a five-minute interval service could not be turned round reliably off one platform at Victoria. In normal operation no trams from Bury would be turned at Victoria, so only a single crossover was provided for possible turn-backs from the City direction. It was decided, therefore, to operate a six-minute peak period service and a 12-minute off-peak frequency. Numerous studies have shown that passengers turn-up randomly for frequencies up to 10/12 minutes. For services above 15 minute frequencies passengers target a specific departure. Thus, when Metrolink's Bury-Victoria service opened on 6th April, 1992 the 6/12 minute frequencies were operated with all trams calling at all stops.

The section through Piccadilly Gardens, and particularly that under Piccadilly Railway Station, took longer to complete than had been anticipated, largely because of BR's demands. It was decided, therefore, that the Bury-Victoria service should be extended to GMex. This happened on 27th April, 1992 when the first new street-running tramway in Britain, for over 40 years, was opened. On 15th June the Metrolink service was extended through to Altrincham. Immediately it tapped a previously unserved and unspotted market for cross-Manchester travel.

When the service was extended from both Victoria and St Peter's Square to Piccadilly on 17th July 1992, it was apparent that the all-day through/direct service could not be abandoned, although not a contractual commitment. Thus, the service pattern was established: Bury-Piccadilly-Altrincham every 12 minutes and Bury-direct-Altrincham every 12 minutes, providing an all-day six-minute service between Bury and the City Centre, Altrincham and the City Centre. Passengers were not allowed to remain on the tram as it reversed in the undercroft at Piccadilly, so today the Bury-Piccadilly and Altrincham-Piccadilly are shown as separate services. The direct service is also shown as a separate service, as are the Eccles and Media City UK services.

The line from St Werburgh's Road in Chorlton to Victoria opened in July 2011, being extended to Oldham Mumps on 13th June 2012. The service is scheduled to be extended to Rochdale Railway Station during 2013.

Eventually, a six-minute peak service will be introduced from Shaw and Crompton, terminating at St Werburgh's Road, until services are extended beyond there to East Didsbury.

In due time all trams from Rochdale and Shaw and Crompton will operate through Oldham Town Centre, each on a 12-minute all-day frequency, co-ordinated to provide a six-minute frequency from Shaw and Crompton to St Werburgh's Road. Eventually, one of the St Werburgh's Road terminating services will be extended to East Didsbury (with the ultimate aim of reaching Stockport). It is not yet clear where the other St Werburgh's Road service will terminate, nor where the Airport service will originate. The Airport line is scheduled to open in 2016.

The Bury-Piccadilly service was extended to Droylsden on 11th February 2013. In due course it is planned to extend the Altrincham-Piccadilly service to Ashton. Meanwhile, the Eccles service will continue to terminate at Piccadilly, eventually using the centre turnback siding that has been built just outside the Undercroft. It is also proposed to cut back the Media City UK service to Cornbrook where the layout has been modified to permit such an operation. Cornbrook can now turn back trams from either direction. It is a little surprising that the largely segregated (and hence more reliable) Bury and Altrincham to Piccadilly services have been linked to the street-running Droylsden/Ashton service when the largely street-running services from Eccles and Media City UK would seem to be the more obvious candidates. Only time will tell if this was the best decision.

The much-talked-about service to the Trafford Centre, which would leave the Eccles line at Pamona, has to be financed entirely by the private sector. In any event, it would not come in until after completion of all the Phase 3b works.

The pattern of Metrolink services thus established will be:

Bury-Piccadilly-Droylsden
Bury-Atrincham
Altrincham-Piccadilly-Ashton-under-Lyne
(Rochdale)-Shaw & Crompton-Oldham-St Werurgh's Road
Eccles-Piccadilly
Media City UK-Cornbrook shuttle

Following the dubious decision to close Mosley Street stop, interchange between services can take place at Piccadilly Gardens, St Peter's Square and Cornbrook. If you are not travelling on a through service to your destination, you can usually step-back a tram to make your connection or to change direction. The closure of the Mosley Street stop awaits the installation of the passenger information system (linked to the TMS) to advise passengers as to where the next Altrincham departure goes from: Market Street or Piccadilly Gardens. The additional passengers on these already crowded island platforms must raise some questions.

Victoria Station is to be remodelled with works that were scheduled to start in October 2012 and due for completion in summer 2014. These works are to be undertaken by Network Rail, working to the PTE's specification. Initial works have begun as this book goes to press. During this period the contractors are requested to provide a minimum capacity of 15 trams per hour (tph) in each direction. Since the Bury line requires 10tph, this means that the Oldham Loop will, initially, be limited to 5 tph, ie 12 minute intervals. It must be assumed that this reduced, initial service will operate from Rochdale Railway Station, with no short-workings from Shaw and Crompton. It is hoped to open the service from Rochdale Railway Station on 28th February 2013.

TfGM has completed a consultation on the Second City Crossing, which is planned to go from Victoria via Corporation Street, Cross Street, skirting Albert Square at its east end, to a rebuilt stop at St Peter's Square. Clearly, the addition of such a major facility will allow the re-routing of some Victoria-Deansgate/Castlefield trams. As commented upon previously, breaking established travel patterns is unwise and difficult. One could envisage splitting Bury-Altrincham direct services between the two routes, or routing the Rochdale/Shaw and Crompton originating services over the second line. Time will tell.

The conversion of the Oldham-Rochdale line is a major development in the Metrolink network and a worthy successor to the foundations laid down by the Lancashire & Yorkshire Railway all those years ago.

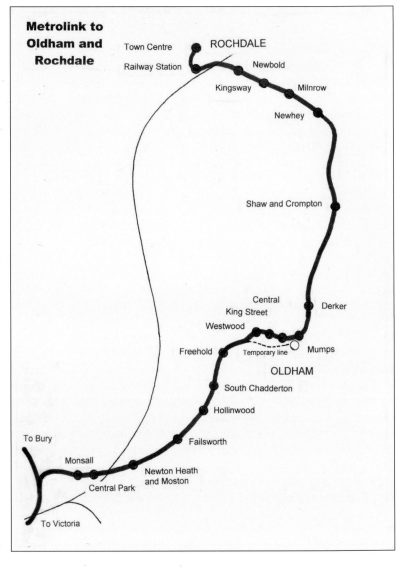

Below left:. Metrolink is open as far as Oldham and unit number 3012 stands at Freehold on a journey from St Werburgh's Road. *(CR)*

Below right:. Later the same day , number 3012 is seen again about to leave South Chadderton for Oldham. *(DSH)*

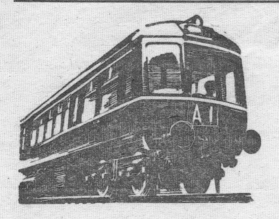

Special Excursion

BY

DIESEL TRAIN

WINDERMERE

SUNDAY 14th MAY 1961

FROM	DEPARTURE TIMES	RETURN FARES SECOND CLASS	RETURN ARRIVAL TIMES
	am	s d	pm
HOLLINWOOD	9 30		9 38
OLDHAM WERNETH	9 35		9 35
„ CENTRAL	9 38	15/6	9 32
„ MUMPS	9 41		9 29
SHAW	9 48		9 22
ROCHDALE	9 58	14/–	9 12
CASTLETON	10 2	14/–	9 8
HEYWOOD	10 7	13/6	9 1
BURY KNOWSLEY STREET	10 15	13/–	8 52
BOLTON TRINITY STREET	10 28	12/–	8 39
CHORLEY	10 50	10/–	8 21
PRESTON	11 10	8/9	8 2

WINDERMERE TOWN arrive 12 25 pm

Return from WINDERMERE TOWN at 6 55 pm

SPECIAL NOTICE

Tickets for this Excursion will be Strictly Limited to the Seating Capacity of the train and passengers are requested to Book their tickets in advance.

Children under Three Years of age Free : Three Years and under Fourteen, Half-Fare
(Fractions of a penny reckoned as a penny.)

TICKETS CAN BE OBTAINED IN ADVANCE AT THE STATIONS AND OFFICIAL RAILWAY AGENTS

Further information will be supplied on application to the Stations, Official Railway Agents, or to Mr. T. W. POLDING, District Passenger Manager, L.M.R., Hunts Bank, Manchester 3. Tel. BLA 3456, Ext. 382.

April 1961

XB/HD

BR 35000

Kirkham & Pratt Ltd. Mcr. 4.

E 282/HD

APPENDIX A
Acts of Parliament authorising phase one of the Manchester-Oldham-Rochdale conversion works

Greater Manchester (Light Rapid Transit System) Act 1988. (Manchester City Centre)

Greater Manchester (Light Rapid Transit System) (Number 2) Act 1988. ((Bury and Altrincham)

Greater Manchester (Light Rapid Transit System) Act 1990. (Salford Quays)

Greater Manchester (Light Rapid Transit System) (Number 2) Act 1990. (Dumplington, Chorlton, Oldham, Rochdale, Cornbrook Junction and Salford Quays)

Greater Manchester (Light Rapid Transit System) Act 1991. (Rochdale town centre, East Didsbury, Salford Quays and Bury)

Greater Manchester (Light Rapid Transit System) Act 1992. (Trafford Park, Oldham, Rochdale and Manchester city centre)

Greater Manchester (Light Rapid Transit System) Act 1994. (Oldham Town Centre)

APPENDIX B
List of stations between Manchester, Oldham and Rochdale and distances in miles from Victoria and Rochdale

Read down		Read up
0	VICTORIA	14.75
	Monsall (a)	
	Central Park (a)	
1	Miles Platting (closed)	13.25
2.75	Dean Lane (b)	12
3.75	Failsworth	11
4.75	Hollinwood	10
	South Chadderton (a)	
	Freehold (a)	
6.5	Werneth (closed 3/10/09)	8.25
7.25	Oldham Central (closed 18/04/66)	7.5
7.5	Oldham Mumps	7.25
8.0	Derker (opened 30/9/85)	6.75
8.5	Royton Junction (closed 8/5/87)	6.25
9.75	Royton (closed 16/04/66)	
10.25	Shaw and Crompton	4.5
12.0	New Hey	2.75
13.0	Milnrow	1.75
	Kingsway (a)	
	Newbold (a)	
14.75	ROCHDALE	0

(a) Built for Metrolink
(b) Renamed 'Newton Heath and Moston' for Metrolink

APPENDIX C
List of signal boxes between Manchester, Oldham and Rochdale

Victoria East Junction

Turntable

Manchester Loop
Footbridge
Cheetham Hill Junction
Smedley Viaduct
Monsall Street

Miles Platting Bank
Newtown No 1
Newtown No 2
Collyhurst Street
Miles Platting
Brewery Sidings

Thorpes Bridge Junction
Dean Lane
Failsworth
Hollinwood
Werneth No 1
Werneth No 2
Oldham No 1
Oldham No 2
Oldham No 3
Hartford Sidings
Royton Junction
Royton Junction Sidings
Shaw South
Shaw North
Crompton Sidings
Jubilee Sidings
New Hey
Milnrow
Buckley Hill
Rochdale East Junction

In April 1961 Fowler 2-6-2T number 40063 stands alongside Turntable box while acting as Bay Platform Pilot at Victoria. *(IGH)*

APPENDIX D
The last steam timetable winter 1957/58

Table 147—

MANCHESTER, MIDDLETON, OLDHAM, ROYTON AND ROCHDALE

WEEKDAYS

Stations (top to bottom):
MANCHESTER (Victoria) ...... dep
Miles Platting
Newton Heath
Moston
MIDDLETON JUNCTION ...... arr
MIDDLETON
CASTLETON
Dean Lane, Newton Heath
Failsworth
Hollinwood
OLDHAM (Werneth)
(Central)
(Mumps) { arr / dep
Royton Junction
ROYTON ...... arr
Shaw and Crompton ...... dep
New Hey
Milnrow
ROCHDALE ...... arr

WEEKDAYS—continued

Table 147—
continued

MANCHESTER, MIDDLETON, OLDHAM, ROYTON AND ROCHDALE

WEEKDAYS—continued

WEEKDAYS—continued / **SUNDAYS**

For notes see page 390

For other Train Services between Manchester (Victoria) and Miles Platting, see Table 119.

B Arrives 12 17 p.m. on Saturdays.
C—Arrives six minutes earlier.
MO—Mondays only
SO—Saturdays only.
SX—Saturdays excepted.
MSX—Mondays and Saturdays excepted

Table 147

APPENDIX E
The full dmu timetable winter 1961/62

Table 147 — MANCHESTER TO MIDDLETON, OLDHAM, ROYTON AND ROCHDALE

353

352

51

A tribute to steam

Two views of the Stevenson Locomotive Society / Manchester Locomotive Society's 'Old Manchester Tour' in May 1956. The train tackles the Werneth Incline double-headed by two Aspinall locomotives, 2-4-2T 50647 piloting 0-6-0 52438. *(Both DLC)*

Summer 1961. Chester-based BR standard class 4-6-0 number 73071 is seen above passing Heyside with empty stock off a Butlins special from Pen-y-Chain. *(IGH)*

Double-heading of extras brought a diversity of visiting engines to the Oldham Loop. A Failsworth to Blackpool excursion dashes through Milnrow behind Stanier 2-6-4T number 42623 of Accrington shed piloting Carlisle Kingmoor's Black 5 4-6-0 number 45317. *(IGH)*

A Patriot on the Oldham line. Seen below: passing Heyside running tender first is number 45517, an un-named member of the class. It provides power for a returning holiday extra from Bridlington to Oldham and would have run round its train of ex-LNER coaches at Rochdale. Number 45517 was a Liverpool Bank Hall-based engine and was a regular performer on Liverpool to Newcastle expresses, but a rarity on the branch. *(IGH)*

Two evocative views of what was Royton Junction in the early sixties. Above a Fowler class 3 2-6-2T number 40014 departs with a Rochdale to Victoria local consisting of a 4-coach rake of BR standard non-corridor coaches, while below a pick-up freight stands in the up yard headed by Fowler class 7F 0-8-0 number 49618, a generally unpopular LMS development of the former LNWR-designed G2. *(Both PH)*

A returning holiday excursion from North Wales is photographed above between Oldham Central and Mumps. The heavy train required double-heading over the steep gradients of the loop. Shortly to be withdrawn, Aspinall class 3F 0-6-0 number 52114 pilots Stanier class 5 4-6-0 number 45189 of Crewe South shed. *(RSG)*

Excursion trains always provided a great deal of interest for railway photographers in the sixties. On the right are two more examples seen passing Heyside between Royton and Shaw in September 1962. In the upper picture 1T69, the 10.30 from Hollinwood to Blackpool is made up of a typically mixed bag of coaches with Hughes 'Crab' 2-6-0 number 42709 of Newton Heath piloting its shedmate Stanier 'Jubilee' 4-6-0 number 45661 'Vernon'.

In the lower view on the following day, 1T61, the 11.24 Shaw to Morecambe is pictured hauled by another Newton Heath 'Jubilee', number 45710 'Invincible'. *(Both PH)*

The largest steam locomotives to work over the line were the BR Standard 7MT Britannia 4-6-2s. On a wet 20th June 1964 number 70045 'Lord Rowallen', at the head of a Shaw to Blackpool holiday extra, crosses a new dmu. *(IGH)*

On the left, in similar dismal weather, a returning holiday train from Morecambe to Oldham calls at Shaw behind one of the rare and unsuccessful Metrovick-built Co-Bo diesels. *(RSG)*

Below: on the last day of double line running between Shaw and Rochdale, two class 104s stand side by side in a dilapidated Shaw station. The notice tells passengers that trains in both directions will use the old Manchester platform on the left. This would cause much confusion and the Rochdale platform was reinstated with trains terminating at Shaw once more using the crossover in the foreground to regain the inward platform. *(Both RSG)*

Coal in large quantities was tripped from Royton Junction Down sidings to Higginshaw gas works. The steep incline into the works limited the maximum load. On an even wetter 27th March 1965 the Locomotive Club of Great Britain organised a brake van trip for members to travel the short branch. *(IGH)*

Below: a class 110 Calder Valley 3-car dmu approaches Werneth on the line from Hollinwood, while on the incline itself is the very last train; another brake van trip organised by the Locomotive Club of Great Britain on 5th January 1963. The locomotive, 8F 2-8-0, number 48546, has slipped to a standstill in the snow and is waiting rear end assistance, eventually provided by a WD 2-8-0. *(IGH)*

The early diesels

Above: A six-car special for the Pope's visit to Manchester, made up of 1957-built Birmingham RCW type 104 units heads southward under Bridge Street and past Dunwood Park between New Hey and Shaw. *(JD)*

Left upper: A hybrid dmu stands in the through platforms at Manchester Victoria formed of a Gloucester Railway Carriage and Wagon works power car and one of the original Cravens units. This combination became more familiar as the Cravens became increasingly unreliable. *(PD)*

Left lower: On a winter's day a Derby-built unit approaches New Hey station with a Rochdale to Manchester service.

Above: In the summer of 1990 a Brush class 31 diesel stands in Shaw station with the 10.03 Rochdale to Blackpool North via Oldham. Meanwhile, Pacer unit 142001 is about to leave forming the 09.45 Manchester Victoria to Rochdale. *(JD)*

Right upper: Another class 31 hauls a set of mixed liveried coaches on another Blackpool train approaching Shaw. This was during the period when Network North West introduced through services from Rochdale to Blackpool or Southport via Oldham and Manchester Victoria. *(RSG)*

Right lower: Heyside, the first bit of open country on the Oldham Loop, lay between Royton Junction and Shaw. During the Network North West era of 1990 there were three diesel loco-hauled trains a day each way over the line from Rochdale to Blackpool. Most trains were pulled by a variety of class 31s but on this occasion the train is powered by an English Electric class 37 locomotive. *(RSG)*

Above: With the ridge of Oldham Edge in the background, a 2-car class 120 unit passes Shaw signal box on a Manchester to Rochdale working in July 1982. Originally built as 4- or 6-car sets for inter-city services on the Western Region, it was very rare to see them in this formation. *(JD)*

Opposite page upper: A Llandudno to Oldham holiday extra comprising three 2-car class 108 units, a pair of Metro-Cammell class 101s and a rare 2-car Park Royal class 103, making up the maximum dmu formation of 12 cars, approaches Heyside. *(RSG)*

Opposite page lower: An unusual visitor to the branch, a Neville Hill-based Calder Valley class 110 unit pauses at Shaw, while on the down platform a Greater Manchester-liveried class 142 is about to leave for Rochdale. *(JD)*

Right upper: Two GMPTE orange-painted Pacers cross at Shaw on a pleasant summer evening. The up (right) train is continuing beyond Victoria to Wigan, thus providing a cross-Manchester service which will serve Salford. *(RSG)*

Lower right: The 13.59 from Rochdale to Kirkby, formed by class 150 Sprinter number 150147, is seen arriving at Shaw in August 1995. The extension from Wigan Wallgate to Kirkby was to cover a Merseyside PTE service which provided an end-to-end connection at Kirkby with the Mersey Electrics through to Liverpool. *(PH)*

Trains of many colours

Left upper: In Greater Manchester PTE orange livery a class 142 Pacer approaches Oldham Mumps station from Victoria, en route to Shaw. The brick-built station buildings can be seen above the cab of the leading vehicle of the train and the 'H' layout of the station itself can be clearly seen on the right. The date is 18th August 1985. *(PH)*

Left centre: On 3rd May 1986 another Pacer unit is pictured at the same spot with the 10.30 Manchester Victoria to Rochdale train. This unit is in the Provincial Services livery following the sectorisation of the railways. *(PH)*

Left lower: Another class 142 pacer, still in Great Western livery following its recent transfer to the cold North West, is seen here in wintery weather soon after leaving New Hey for Rochdale.

Opposite page upper: A two-car class 155 Sprinter in Metro (West Yorkshire PTE) livery rolls into Shaw on a Manchester to York working. This service usually took the direct line to Rochdale via Castleton but was diverted by to Oldham Loop due to Sunday engineering work. Following an initiative by STORM the opportunity was taken to insert stops at Mumps and Shaw to test the demand for a regular service. *(RSG)*

Opposite page lower: A class 153 single-car Sprinter turns back at Shaw ready for its return trip to Victoria. It is in Regional Railways livery, the new name for Provincial Services. The 153s were created by dividing the class 155 units. *(RSG)*

Opposite page upper: The 08.34 Southport to Rochdale service is seen approaching Oldham Mumps formed by Pacer unit number 142029. The unit is in Regional Railways North West livery. *(PH)*

Opposite page lower: Another Pacer unit number 142064 in Regional Railways colours but with a Network North West decal on the side, seen here at Shaw and Crompton with the 14.29 service from Rochdale to Wigan Wallgate on 4th August 1985. *(PH)*

Three successive up departures from Derker on a pleasant summer day, 18th August 1995.*)*

Right upper: The 14.29 from Rochdale to Wigan Wallgate formed by number 142055 in yellow MerseyRail livery. *(PH)*

Right middle: The 14.18 from Shaw and Crompton to Bolton service in provided by single coach Sprinter number 153367. *(PH)*

Right lower: The 14.48 Shaw and Crompton to Clitheroe working formed by class 156 Super Sprinter number 156429. *(PH)*

The Last Days

Above: On 29th July 2009 class 142 Pacer unit number 142067 has just arrived in bay platform 2 at Victoria ready to work the12.38 all stations back to Shaw. *(CR)*

Left: On the same day Sprinter unit number 150140 stands in platform 2 in a haze of exhaust fumes while waiting to leave on the 12.24 to Rochdale. Metrolink unit number 1007 stands in the Bury line platform on the left. *(CR)*

Opposite page upper: Sprinter number 150277 runs into Dean Lane with the 11.38 all stations Victoria to Shaw. Newton Heath Traction Maintenance Depot is visible through the arch of Dean Lane bridge. *(CR)*

Opposite page Lower: An unidentified Pacer unit approaches Dean Lane forming the 11.31 express from Rochdale and passes the Newton Heath Refuse Destructor plant from where regular trains run to the landfill site at Appley Bridge near Wigan. *(CR)*

Above: The 16.21 from Shaw, worked by Pacer unit number 142052 runs into Failsworth on 22nd June 2009. *(CR)*

Left: Another view of the same set waiting for the signal to leave. *(CR)*

*Opposite page upper:*Evening shadows lengthen as an unknown Pacer unit crosses the Rochdale Canal at Wrigley Head between Failsworth and Hollinwood with the 18.21 from Shaw to Victoria in July 2009. Only a few years previously this sylvan view was a scene of industrial dereliction. *(CR)*

Opposite page lower: Pacer unit number142039 crosses the M60 Manchester outer ring road and approaches Hollinwood with the 17.56 Rochdale to Victoria on 8th June 2009. *(CR)*

Opposite page upper: Sprinter 150277 emerges from Werneth tunnel and hurries through Werneth station with the 10.56 Rochdale to Manchester express on 22nd July 2009. *(CR)*

Opposite page lower: On the same day a class 150/1 Sprinter approaches Oldham with the 10.09 Victoria to Shaw. The once extensive Waterloo sidings on the left are now covered by mature trees and the former mills and gas works on the right of the line have now given way to Oldham Way, the town's inner ring road. *(CR)*

Above: Despite the impending closure of the line, staff have still looked after the flower beds at the south end of Oldham Mumps. *(CR)*

Right upper: Unusual motive power for the loop, Class 156 unit number 156471 waits its time at Oldham Mumps before leaving for Rochdale. *(CR)*

Right middle: Pacer number 142008 stands in the down platform, ready to leave with the 10.38 from Manchester to Shaw. *(CR)*

Right lower: Class 150/1 number 150143 arrives at Mumps with the 10.51 all stations from Shaw to Manchester. The original wrought iron and glass roof is still intact and Oldham is one of the three remaining manned stations on the loop, the others being Rochdale and Shaw. *(CR)*

Above: Derker station in July 2009 with a class 142 Pacer arriving on a Shaw to Victoria stopping journey. The bridge carrying Yates Street over the line rises up to the left, the left hand arch crossing over the site of the tracks giving access to the former Westwood yard which was located between the trees seen through the right hand arch. *(CR)*

Left upper: On a hot August day the hay has already been gathered in as Pacer number 142091, newly transferred to Newton Heath from the Cardiff Valleys and still carrying Arriva Wales livery, approaches Bullcote Lane bridge with the 11.09 from Manchester to Shaw. This rural stretch between Derker and Shaw is the highest point on the line. *(CR)*

Left lower: Pacer number150146 stands at the up starter at Shaw ready to work the 11.51 stopping service to Manchester Victoria. The former Briar Mill, now industrial units, towers in the background. *(CR)*

Turning back at Shaw

Right upper: Newton Heath Pacer unit number142014 approaches Shaw station on 20th May 2009 on the 10.38 from Manchester Victoria.

Right middle: Shaw was the end of the double line, the outward track continuing for a short distance as a reversing facility for trains turning back there. Having waited its time, 142014 crosses over on to the up platform to work back to Manchester. *(CR)*

Right lower: And finally 142014 crosses Beal Lane and passes the signal box with the 11.21 all stations to Victoria. *(CR)*

Below: Notice of Conversion on the up platform at Shaw.

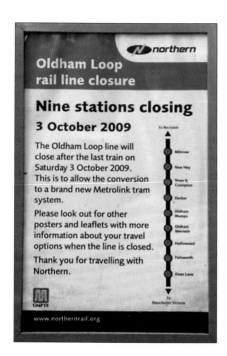

73

Pacer unit number 142052 leaves New Hey with the 11.56 service from Rochdale to Manchester on 25th June 2009. The inbound journey has originated at Wigan Wallgate and has worked through via Manchester and Castleton. *(CR)*

Left: The station sign on Huddersfield Road shows New Hey. *(CR)*

NEWHEY OR NEW HEY?

There has always been some doubt as to how it should be spelled. The Ordnance Survey has called it both from time to time. The railways, as far back as Lancashire and Yorkshire days at least, called it New Hey and both Manchester Corporation and the North Western Road Car Company showed New Hey on their buses, but Rochdale Corporation always used Newhey. The PTE could never make up its mind and used New Hey for railway publicity and Newhey for buses, sometimes both in the same publication. Metrolink refers to it as Newhey so we have used New Hey when referring to heavy rail operation and Newhey for Metrolink.

Above: Pacer number142047 passes under Elizabethan Way and runs into Milnrow on 6th June 2009 as the 13.31 from Rochdale to Manchester Victoria. The neglected state of the line with Harbour Lane bridge in the foreground and the abandoned and overgrown down platform on the left is clearly shown. *(CR)*

On 5th August 2009 an unidentified class 142 unit crosses the Rochdale Canal forming the 09.56 Victoria to Rochdale. *(CR)*

Opposite page upper: An unidentified class 142 unit forming the 10.31 Rochdale to Manchester service crosses Milnrow Road on 5th August 2009. *(CR)*

Opposite page lower: Having come off the Oldham branch on to the up line at Rochdale North junction, Newton Heath Pacer unit number 142062 has crossed over to the down line and runs into the bay platform with the 13.54 from Manchester on 28th May 2009. *(CR)*

Right upper: On the last day of operation Class 156 unit 156441 stands in the bay platform at Rochdale with the 10.31 departure for Manchester Victoria via Oldham *(CR)*

Right middle: Earlier in the day number 156466 was named Gracie Fields at a ceremony at Manchester Victoria. *(CR)*

Right lower: The end of the line. On the following day the bay platform at Rochdale stands deserted. *(CR)*

Below:: Last day tickets *(LYRS/DLC)*

Northern Rail
Oldham Loop Last Train 3rd October 2009
MANCHESTER TO
ROCHDALE
VIA OLDHAM MUMPS
SOUVENIR TICKET | STANDARD CLASS

031009 · NOT VALID FOR TRAVEL

Class	Ticket type		Adult	Child	
STD	ANYTIME DAY S		ONE	NIL	SCL
	Start date		Number		
PRIU	03·OCT·09		02576	4633ө9654-7D	
From	Valid until				Price
MANCHESTER STNS	03·OCT·09				£0·95M
To	Route		Validity		
ROCHDALE *	ANY PERMITTED		ON DATE SHOWN		
					SINGLE

Printed 20·51 on 03·OCT·09

Rebuilding

New Metrolink M5000 car number 3003 stands in Queens Road depot on 20th September 2009 soon after delivery. Despite the indicator display, the occasion was a visit by the Greater Manchester Group of the Chartered Institute of Transport. The Rochdale line would be served exclusively by these units. *(CR)*

Above: Tram number 3010 passes through Victoria on a test run on 9th February 2010. On the left is a Northern Rail class 158 unit forming the 10.48 departure to Leeds and Selby. *(CR)*

Right: The Oldham and Rochdale branch leaves the Bury line at Irk Valley Junction and follows the long-disused viaduct which can be seen in the left upper background, curving down hill to join the former loop line just before the bridge over Smedley Road. In this picture, taken from Collyhurst Road bridge in September 2010, the sides of the bridge are covered in white polythene sheeting to protect road users Below: while it is refurbished. The ballasting is nearly complete and the columns for the overhead are in place. *(CR)*

At Thorpes Bridge Junction the Rochdale direct line goes straight on while the Oldham branch forks right. In the V is Newton Heath Diesel Maintenance depot on the site of the former steam depot 26A. The new Metrolink alignment is to the right of the junction and in this view taken from Thorp Road bridge in August 2011 the track is being laid and the OHLE is in course of erection. *(DSH)*

Typifying the extent of the rebuilding work needed on the existing stations on the line is Failsworth. The pictures below show on the left the neglected and overgrown entrance which was a feature of the last years, while on the right can be seen the building of the new lift and stairs. *(CR)*

At Shaw, in order to minimise the effect of the increase in train movements from four to ten an hour, the new tram stop has been resited to the south of Beal Lane level crossing. Taken on a freezing 23rd February 2012, the photographs show the site of the now demolished former station and work proceeding on the new tram stop.

Alternate trams will turn back at Shaw and Crompton and a bay platform will be provided which will make the stop the only one with on the system with more than two platforms. *(CR)*

Above: The entrance to Milnrow Station in June 2009. *(CR)*

Right upper:
Milnrow tram stop with work in progress in February 2012. *(CR)*

Right lower: On 18th May 2011 the single span bridge over the Rochdale Canal has been removed, the double track replacement has been dropped into place and final work is in progress on the bridge supports and embankment. *(CR)*

Opposite page upper: Newhey tram stop takes shape in February 2012. *(CR)*

Opposite page lower: In this view looking north from Newhey Road bridge in June 2009 the track has been lifted and drainage work is in progress. Elizabethan Way runs parallel with the the line. *(CR)*

Above: By November 2011 work on the new Metrolink stop outside Rochdale railway station was progressing. The imposing building in the left background is St John's Church. *(CR)*

Left: In February 2012 track laying is under way on High Level Road which the new line uses to drop down from the railway viaduct to street level. *(CR)*

Opposite page upper: In September 2012 the platforms of the new tram stop are now taking shape. *(CR)*

Opposite page lower: Two months later, with a deadline for opening in February 2013, the platforms are nearing completion. *(CR)*

Metrolink

The line opened to the temporary terminus at Oldham Mumps on 13th June 2012 and was extended to Shaw and Crompton on 16th December. Tram number 3045 was photographed working through to Rochdale some weeks later, on a busy Easter Saturday afternoon. *(JAS)*

North from Victoria

Trams to Oldham and Rochdale follow the Bury line out of Victoria and, after passing under the four-track heavy rail route up Miles Platting bank, emerge from Collyhurst tunnel and cross the valley of the River Irk on the skew bow lattice Irk Valley Viaduct. This was the scene of the accident in August 1953 when a Manchester to Bury electric train collided with a steam engine and plunged into the valley below. At Irk Valley Junction, immediately after leaving the viaduct, trams for Oldham swing away to the right and run down hill to join the former loop line at Smedley Viaduct Junction, as can be seen in the driver's view on the right.

In the lower view from the driver's cab an inward tram approaches the junction from the opposite direction while older T68A tram number 1028 passes on an outward Bury service. This was one of the trams built in 1992 for the original Bury-Altrincham line Metrolink conversion and subsequently fitted with cab air conditioning, the control unit being visible on the cab roof. *(Both DSH)*

Below: Manchester-bound unit number 3015 emerges from under Collyhurst Road bridge and negotiates Smedley Viaduct Junction on an Oldham to St Werburgh's Road working. The spur to Queens Road depot bears away to the right on the track of the former loop line. Compare this picture with the 1925 view from the same location on page 13 and the construction scene on page 79. *(CR)*

The Manchester Loop Line

Left upper: The first stop out of Victoria on the former loop line is Monsall. In the early morning sunshine tram number 3011 arrives at the inward platform on its way to St Werburgh's Road. *(CR)*

Left middle: The Monsall tram stop is situated in a deep cutting in the middle of a new housing development. Under a threatening September sky unit number 3001 emerges from Monsall Street bridge and runs into the outward platform on its way to Oldham. *(CR)*

Right upper: View from the cab of an outward tram arriving at Central Park. *(DSH)*

The futuristic station at Central Park, intended to be the flagship of the new line, was completed in 2005 but due to the withdrawal of funding stood unused for seven years. *(CR)*

Unit number 3029 leaves the outward platform and prepares to cross the spectacular curved bridge over the main lines out of Victoria (above), while below: number 3026 drops down from the bridge and runs into the inward platform on a Manchester-bound working. *(Both CR)*

Through the former Dean Lane station the Metrolink line has been singled (above) to allow the old down track to be retained for use by trains serving the Greater Manchester waste transfer facility further along the line, where unit number 3020 can be seen (right) on its way to St Werburgh's Road. In the picture below number 3021 waits in the bi-directional platform at the new Newton Heath and Moston tram stop before leaving for St Werburgh's Road. *(DSH above, CR below and right)*

On a sunny June afternoon unit number 3027 runs into the new Failsworth tram stop with a working from Oldham. *(CR)*

*Lower left:*On the same day unit number 3024 crosses the M60 motorway and approaches Hollinwood on a journey from Oldham to St Werburgh's Rd. *(CR)*

Right lower: Once a picture of industrial dereliction, the view from the platform end at the new South Chadderton stop looks positively rural as unit 3027 approaches down the hill on its way from Oldham. *(CR)*

On a Manchester-bound working, number 3027 stands (above) at the new Freehold stop as passengers talk to the driver. Once the largest cotton mill in Oldham, the now derelict Hartford Mill rises up in the background. *(CR)*

Immediately after passing under Featherstall Road bridge the Oldham Town Centre diversion will turn sharp left, the slab base already in place. The temporary Metrolink route continues straight on through the site of the now demolished Werneth station towards Werneth tunnel which can be seen in the distance. A plinth above the portal carries the crest of the then newly formed Lancashire and Yorkshire Railway. In preparation for Metrolink the original BR track was welded up, realigned and tamped instead of being completely re-laid as was done elsewhere as, under current plans, it has no long term future after the Town Centre section opens. Fortunately, the two tunnels on this part of the route provided sufficient clearance for the 750v overhead wire although a 25Kv supply for a heavy rail conversion would have needed costly engineering work. Compare this view with the picture on page 17 taken from the same spot. *(DSH)*

Tram number 3026 runs under the rebuilt footbridge into the temporary terminus at Oldham Mumps on the last few yards of its journey from St Werburgh's Road. *(CR)*

Above and below: Until the route through Oldham Town Centre is opened, the area is being served by a temporary tram stop on the old line just to the west of the former Mumps railway station and linked to the town centre by a footpath across waste land. Tram number 3025 has just left the platform and is heading up the line to the crossover before returning to the southbound platform as its passengers set off on the long trek to civilisation. *(CR above, DSH below)*

Above: Under a threatening Pennine sky tram number 3022 negotiates the crossover at the end of the line and returns to the temporary stop before working back to St Werburgh's Road. *(Both CR)*

Right: A taste of things to come. Night-time test running started between Oldham and Shaw in October 2012. In the evocative picture on the right a still un-numbered unit is seen at Derker. *(MEN)*

Through to Chorlton

Operationally, trams from Oldham run across Manchester City Centre along the South Manchester line to Chorlton (St Werburgh's Road). The line opened on 7 July 2011 with services running as far as a temporary terminus at Manchester Victoria.

The line leaves the Altrincham route immediately west of Trafford Bar station, the outward track swinging away southwards as can be seen in the upper picture, while the inward track passes underneath the Altrincham line by a long-disused bridge, which can just be seen in the middle picture, before curving sharply upwards to join it just short of the platform at Trafford Bar in the middle distance. The points were laid in during a track possession in the summer of 2009.

From here the route follows the track bed of the former Cheshire Lines Committee route which passed through the short tunnel, the mouth of which can be seen below left, before joining the Manchester Central to Liverpool line at Throstle Nest East Junction near Cornbrook.

At the bottom right a tram bound for St Werburgh's Road has gained the CLC line and is approaching the entrance to the Trafford depot. *(All DSH)*

93

The first stop on the line is at Firswood in the middle of an area of inter-war housing. Tram number 3005 is pictured above arriving on a working to St Werburgh's Road. *(CR)*

Next is Chorlton on the site of the old Chorlton-cum-Hardy railway station. Unit Number 3003 is shown in the upper picture en route to St Werburgh's Road, and later below on its way back to Manchester. *(Both CR)*

Above unit number 3005 runs into the terminus under St.Werburgh's Road bridge. The lift and stairs from the road down to track level can be seen on the right of the arch. *(CR)*

On the right number 3001 has run down to the end of the line, the driver has changed ends and it is now crossing over to the inward line while in the bottom picture it stands at the inward platform ready for it's return journey.

St Werburgh's Road stop is built on the site of the former Chorlton Junction which once marked the end of CLC ownership. The path curving away to the left beyond the brick building is the one-time Great Central route to Guide Bridge which, apart from a local service, was once traversed by the Harwich Boat Express from Liverpool to the East Coast port.

Ahead, beyond the temporary buffer stop, the Metrolink extension to East Didsbury is being built on the bed of the former Midland Railway line through the Peak to Derby and St Pancras. *(Both CR)*

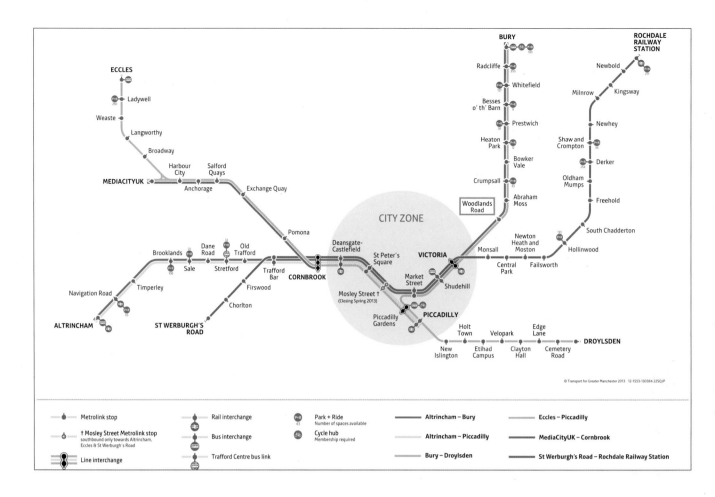

The diagram above, from Transport for Greater Manchester shows the situation at the date of publication with trams running from St Werburgh's Road to Rochdale Railway Station, and from Bury to Droylsden. *(TfGM)*

In the photograph by the author, below, at the bottom of Drake Street the line will curve right into Smith Street to its final terminus at the Transport Interchange. Rochdale town centre with its magnificent Town Hall forms a backdrop to the construction works. *(CR)*